Z O O G R A P H I E S

ZOOGRAPHIES

THE QUESTION OF THE ANIMAL
FROM HEIDEGGER TO DERRIDA

Matthew Calarco

COLUMBIA UNIVERSITY PRESS   NEW YORK

COLUMBIA UNIVERSITY PRESS

Publishers Since 1893

NEW YORK CHICHESTER, WEST SUSSEX

Library of Congress Cataloging-in-Publication Data

Calarco, Matthew, 1972–

Zoographies : the question of the animal from Heidegger to Derrida /
Matthew Calarco.

p. cm.

Includes bibliographical references and index.

ISBN 978-0-231-14022-5 (cloth : alk. paper) — ISBN 978-0-231-14023-2
(pbk. : alk. paper) — ISBN 978-0-231-51157-5 (e-book : alk. paper)

1. Animals (Philosophy)—History—20th century. I. Title

B105.A55C35   2008

179'.3—dc22

2007046991

Columbia University Press books are printed on permanent
and durable acid-free paper.

This book is printed on paper with recycled content.

Designed by Chang Jae Lee

Printed in the United States of America

c 10 9 8 7 6 5 4 3 2 1
p 10 9 8 7 6 5 4 3

CONTENTS

ACKNOWLEDGMENTS

In the course of writing this book, I have been assisted and supported in innumerable ways. I wish especially to thank the following people and institutions: Wendy Lochner for her initial interest in this project and for her generous patience and guidance during the writing and production process; Neil Badmington, Paola Cavalieri, Marc Goodman, Shaheen Moosa, Steven Vogel, and Jason Wirth for reading portions of different chapters and providing me with helpful feedback; two anonymous reviewers for Columbia University Press for their insightful suggestions; and Sweet Briar College Faculty Grants Committee for financial assistance.

I owe a substantial debt of gratitude to two people in particular. Peter Atterton has either read or discussed with me in conversation nearly every idea and argument laid out in this book. I envy his remarkable philosophical and critical abilities and count myself fortunate if even small traces of them have found their way into my writing. Nicole Garrett listened patiently to my ideas and helped me to clarify my thinking on more occasions than I am able to enumerate. Her support of and confidence in my work has sustained me in ways that she will never fully realize and that I can never fully convey. I dedicate this book to her—and the animals, past and present, from whom she and I have learned to live.

I thank the publishers for permission to reprint the following materials:

"Jamming the Anthropological Machine." In *Giorgio Agamben: Sovereignty and Life,* ed. Matthew Calarco and Steven DeCaroli. Stanford, Calif.: Stanford University Press, 2007. © Stanford University Press.

ZOOGRAPHIES

INTRODUCTION

The Question of the Animal

ON PHILOSOPHY AND ANIMAL STUDIES

The present volume, while primarily philosophical in scope and content, was written as a contribution to the emerging interdisciplinary field of animal studies. While there is no widely agreed upon definition of what precisely constitutes animal studies, it is clear that most authors and activists working in the field share the conviction that the "question of the animal" should be seen as one of the central issues in contemporary critical discourse. This conviction stands in stark contrast to the reception the question has had in most individual disciplines in the sciences and humanities. In my home discipline of philosophy, for example, questions concerning animals are typically relegated by Anglo-American philosophers to a subspecialization within the field of environmental ethics, which is itself considered a minor area of applied ethics. Given that the field of applied ethics is, in turn, often viewed as a minor field in philosophy and (more pejoratively) as a distraction from more serious and substantial philosophical pursuits (namely, metaphysics and epistemology), it is no wonder that many philosophers interested in exploring the rich set of issues surrounding animals and "animality" have chosen to do so within the context of the semiautonomous region of animal studies. The main philosophical figures discussed in this volume—who include Martin Heidegger, Emmanuel Levinas, Giorgio Agamben, and Jacques Derrida—belong to an alternative branch of philosophy sometimes referred to as "Continental," or "modern European" philosophy.

This approach to philosophy is characterized by, among many other things, its commitment to existential, ethical, and sociopolitical issues, and it is this "engaged" focus that serves (whether accurately or not) as one of the myriad ways of distinguishing Continental philosophy from its Anglo-American counterpart. It might thus seem that the question of the animal would find a welcome home in Continental philosophy; this has, however, historically been far from the truth.

One of the overarching aims of this book is to argue that the kinds of questions and concerns central to animal studies *should* become more important for philosophy in general and for Continental philosophers in particular, and I will make these arguments in due course. Another point that I hope to make in the pages that follow is that several of the tools, concepts, and theoretical frameworks of Continental philosophy, despite having their origins in a largely anthropocentric context, can make a unique contribution to animal studies, and I shall have much to say on this matter, as well. First, however, it will be useful to explain in a bit more detail what I take to be at stake in the field of animal studies and then explain why I have chosen to use the phrase "the question of the animal" in the subtitle of the book and as an entry point into the arguments made here.

Animal studies, or "human-animal studies" (as it is sometimes called), comprises a wide range of disciplines within the humanities, social sciences, and biological and cognitive sciences. As I just mentioned, there is no standard or widely accepted definition of the field, and its main terms and theoretical foci are still open-ended at this point. I would suggest, however, that the main stakes of the field lie in the effort to place questions concerning animals at the center of critical inquiry. The precise manner in which these questions are framed, debated, and answered depends, of course, to a large extent on the particular field of origin. And yet, despite the disciplinary differences and multiple theoretical approaches in animal studies, there are at least two recurring and structural questions that undergird much of the work being done in the field. One question concerns the being of animals, or "animality," and the other concerns the human-animal distinction.

In view of the concept of "animality" or animal nature, many theorists have questioned whether there actually is a shared essence or set of characteristics binding all animals together. Much like the critique of essentialism in feminism, queer theory, and race studies, theorists in animal studies seek to track the ways in which the concept of "animality" functions to demarcate humans clearly from animals and establish homogeneities among what appear to be radically different forms of animal life. In so doing, they seek to demonstrate that the notion of animality plays more of a constitutive than denotative role in discourses about animals. Although such analysis is often (negatively) associated with postmodernist versions of "linguistic idealism," it is often found, in fact, outside the humanities, especially in biological debates over the nature of species and the construction of taxonomies.[1] Here, too, one finds persuasive arguments that the wide variety of beings referred to as "animal" cannot be reduced to any simple (or even relatively complex) set of shared characteristics.

If debates over animality threaten to send the concept to its ruin, discussions over the human-animal distinction would appear to make good on this threat. In recent years, traditional human-animal distinctions, which posit a radical discontinuity between animals and human beings, have been relentlessly attacked from multiple theoretical, political, and disciplinary perspectives. In the empirical sciences, Darwinism has had the effect of undermining human-animal dichotomies in the name of gradualist continuism. A similar displacement has occurred in the humanities and social sciences, where the traditional marks of the human (articulate speech, knowledge of death, consciousness, and so on) have been shown either to exist in a similar form among nonhuman animals or not to exist among human beings in the manner that traditional discourses had posited.

Inasmuch as the notion of what constitutes animality has traditionally been figured over and against what is supposed to constitute humanity, when the notion of humanity is undercut, then the concept of animality suffers a similar fate. The effect of the displacement of the human-animal distinction is that, today, thought is no longer certain how to proceed in this domain. Should the human-animal distinction be redrawn along different lines? And if so, along which lines, precisely? Or should it be abandoned altogether?

Throughout the following chapters, I interrogate critically the manner in which each of the major theorists under discussion here seeks either to establish or displace the human-animal distinction. One of the chief theses I defend throughout the book is that *the human-animal distinction can no longer and ought no longer to be maintained.* Several arguments (political, ethical, and ontological) will be presented to give support to this thesis, and I hope the reader will find these arguments persuasive. That said, I have no illusions that philosophical arguments alone will suffice to transform our thinking about what we call animals. Philosophy has only a minor role to play in the larger transformation that is necessary to do justice, in thought and life, to animals. Despite its role not being total, I would suggest that philosophy still has a significant and unique role to play. Philosophy, and perhaps philosophy alone at this point, is able to hold open the possibility that thought might proceed otherwise in regard to animals, without the assurances of traditional conceptions of animality and the human-animal distinction. What thought will encounter once reliance upon these categories is surrendered cannot be known in advance; however, it *is* certain that any genuine encounter with what we call animals will occur only from within the space of this surrender. If there are any properly philosophical stakes in the field of animal studies, I would argue that they lie precisely here, in the clearing of the space for the *event* of what we call animals.

THE QUESTION OF THE ANIMAL

I have used the phrase "the question of the animal" in the title of both the book and this introduction, and I should like to explain my decision to do so. First, it should be noted that the phrase is a quotation and citation from Jacques Derrida, and it should be read as signaling my indebtedness to his work, both in terms of Derrida's larger philosophical project and his writings devoted specifically to animals. Derrida uses this phrase often throughout his writings on animals, and specifically in regard to his critical confrontation with Heidegger around this issue. Thus, in using the phrase, I am implicitly underscoring and endorsing the main thrust of his critique of classical philosophical discourses on "the animal."

When Derrida speaks of "the question of the animal," he is referring first of all to the way in which philosophers have traditionally written about animals in reductive and essentialist terms. Rather than acknowledging the disparate modes of being, relation, and language to be found among animals, most philosophers have sought instead to determine what constitutes animality as such, or the being of "The Animal," understood in the general plural. In posing the question of the animal in response to the dominant philosophical tradition, Derrida joins the group of theorists mentioned above, who call into question essentialist accounts of animality. He argues throughout his writings on this topic that essentialist discourse on animals attempts to create homogeneities where only radical heterogeneity can be found. Whether Derrida's discourse is successful in making this argument and whether it provides an alternative way of thinking about heterogeneity among animals are issues I will take up at more length in the chapter devoted to his work. I will say here, however, that I am in general agreement with his critique of the essentialism of the philosophical tradition and that this critical analysis is one of the most important aspects involved in a rigorous posing of the question of the animal.

There is also an ethical dimension to the question of the animal in Derrida's work, if by "ethical" we understand something like Emmanuel Levinas's notion of ethics as being called into question by the face of the other. Derrida's work on animal issues is predicated on the assumption— an assumption that I share and will try to defend in this book—that the face of the Other cannot be delimited a priori to the realm of the human; or, to rephrase the same thought positively, animals of various sorts might have a face, which is to say, animals might call upon and obligate me in ways that I cannot fully anticipate. "The question of the animal" is thus a question deriving from an animal who faces me, an interruption deriving from a singular "animal," an animal whom I face and by whom I am faced and who calls my mode of existence into question.

Beyond the senses intended by Derrida, the phrase "the question of the animal" carries additional meanings in this book. It is also intended to pose the question of whether we know how to think about animals *at all*. Are any of our extant discourses—whether they derive from science or philosophy, from anthropocentric or nonanthropocentric sources— adequate for describing the rich multiplicity of life forms and perspectives found among those beings we call "animal"? One often finds in animal rights discourse a straightforward reliance on scientific accounts of animals in grounding ethical claims about them; for example, scientific evidence of minds in certain animal species is often invoked to bolster claims about animals' subjectivity and moral standing (or, in reverse, scientific evidence is used to deny moral standing to animals). While I have no general issue with the use of scientific and ethical discourses in describing and rethinking human relationships with animals, and will certainly make use of both kinds of discourses throughout the following chapters, I would not want to make the claim that the sciences and philosophy are able to provide us with an exhaustive account of animal life. For not only are the sciences and philosophy (at least partially) limited by their anthropocentric origins, but it is also the case that they are unable to accomplish on their own the revolution in language and thought that is needed to come to grips with the issues surrounding animal life. There is no doubt that we need to think unheard-of thoughts about animals, that we need new languages, new artworks, new histories, even new sciences and philosophies. The field of animal studies is interdisciplinary precisely for this reason: it is seeking out every available resource to aid in the task of working through the question of the animal. Whether extant discourses, however diverse, can accomplish this task without a corresponding transformation in their underlying *ontologies* is a question that will be broached throughout the volume.

The phrase "the question of the animal" is also meant to convey that the issues raised under this rubric are fundamentally open questions, and questions that open onto related philosophical and political concerns. Although this book is focused squarely on ethical, political, and ontological issues concerning animals, it will become clear as the arguments unfold that the question of the animal is but an opening onto a much larger and much richer set of issues that touch more broadly on the limits of the human. As such, I view the question of the animal and the fields of animal ethics and politics as part of the recent explosion of new social movements aimed at radicalizing left-wing politics in its traditional liberal, humanist form. Whereas pro-animal discourse is often presented as an extension and deepening of liberal humanism, I attempt to recast this discourse as a direct *challenge* to liberal humanism and the metaphysical anthropocentrism that underlies it. In making these points, I am explicitly aligning myself and theorists in animal studies who are doing similar work with the new social movements that are seeking to develop a postliberal, posthumanist approach to politics.

THE POLITICS OF ANTHROPOCENTRISM

There has been considerable discussion of late among radical political and cultural theorists about the fragmentation of the left and how best to navigate the troubled political terrain this division has engendered, and it might be thought that by raising the question of the animal in this political context that I am simply further dividing the left and pushing for yet another mode of identity politics. I will explain shortly how I am trying to accomplish something other than producing this effect, but before doing so, I should say that I do believe much of contemporary animal rights discourse and politics is in fact another form of identity politics or has had precisely the effect of further fragmenting the left, both for good and for bad. Many animal rights theorists and activists see themselves as uncovering some sort of fundamental identity (for example, sentience or subjectivity) shared by all animals (or, rather, the animals they believe worthy of ethical and political standing) in order to represent that identity in the political and legal arena. It is precisely in these forums that the interests of animals compete for attention with the interests of individuals represented by various other kinds of identity-based movements. Inasmuch as the lives and deaths of animals figure minimally, if at all, within much of current political and legal debates, I am certainly inclined to support the efforts by animal rights theorists and activists to provide a "voice" for and represent the "interests" of animals. But this approach to animal ethics and politics is fraught with considerable theoretical and ethical difficulties. Not only does it make the claims of animal rights discourse appear as a kind of distinct politics unrelated to other progressive, leftist issues, but it also proceeds on a set of assumptions about what constitutes the proper scope of "animality" and what the "interests" of animals are—both of which are highly contentious issues. Furthermore, much of animal rights discourse labors under the tacit (and contentious) assumption that the fundamental channels of change regarding animals are to be found in existing legal and political institutions.

Animal rights discourse, then, is beset by two rather fundamental difficulties. On the one hand, in order to gain a voice in the political and legal spheres, it is constrained to adopt the language and strategies of identity politics, which in turn further constrain the discourse to establish a concept of animality and animal interests that must be somewhat distinct from the focus and concerns of other forms of identity politics. This situation creates divisions among progressive causes and leads to a kind of isolationist approach to animal rights politics, where animal rights are seen as floating in an empty space distinct from political concerns about, for example, women's rights, environmental justice, or worker's rights (all of which are, on my understanding of the question of the animal, intimately related to animal rights, even if only for contingent historical reasons). The effects of this kind of isolationism have been felt acutely both within and outside animal rights circles. More so than perhaps any other mode of identity politics, animal rights has been largely abandoned by many progressive leftists, who often see animal rights either as a political issue of secondary (or tertiary) importance or as merely a luxury of the bourgeois activist. At the same time, animal rights activists themselves have often adopted the attitude that animal rights issues trump all other political concerns, and in the process have engaged in a number of rather questionable and sometimes politically regressive and conservative strategies in the name of promoting animal rights.

The other difficulty faced by animal rights theorists and activists is a more subtle but equally important one. The difficulty concerns the tacit *anthropocentric* constraints at work in political and legal institutions and how animal rights discourse ends up acceding to and reproducing the constraints that found and sustain these institutions. Thus, it is not just the case that animal rights discourse is overtly constrained to adopt the strategies of identity politics (as we have just seen), it is also more subtly constrained to determine animality and animal identity according to anthropocentric norms and ideals. This problem can be seen clearly in various aspects of animal rights theory and activism. If one looks at the field of philosophy, for example, it is clear the dominant model of animal rights philosophy espoused by Tom Regan seeks to demonstrate that animals are, in many significant ways, the same as human beings. Regan argues that animals are fundamentally identical with human beings in being subjects-of-a-life, that is, subjects with personal preferences, desires, and a stake in how they are treated. While this notion of subjectivity perhaps hold for members of *certain* animal species, Regan acknowledges that scope of animal subjectivity is quite narrow and is probably not to be found among many beings that are often considered to be animals. Strictly speaking, then, Regan's work is not a case for animal rights but for rights for *subjects,* the classical example of which is human beings. And inasmuch as animals manifest morally relevant human, or subjectlike, traits, they are brought under the scope of moral consideration. But why take this approach when it is clear that Regan would prefer to expand the scope of moral consideration well beyond animals who

manifest basic subjectivity? The answer is that moral philosophy functions, by and large, within an implicit anthropocentric, subject-centered
model, and in order to make a case that can gain a hearing within that
model, one has to speak its language and accede to its demands. Of
course, it is precisely that moral model, language, and demands that
have been used to deny animals basic moral standing for centuries, and
it is paradoxical, to say the least, that animal rights theorists have used
the same anthropocentric criteria that have been used to exclude animals from moral concern to include only certain animals within that
scope and to draw only a new, slightly different exclusionary boundary.
It might seem that animal rights would effect a radical displacement of
anthropocentrism and signal the advent of an alternative moral framework, but instead it has more often than not ended up simply producing
a slightly different version of anthropocentrism and subject-centrism.
And the same story could be told for various efforts to bring animals
within the scope of legal and political consideration. In brief, then, the
anthropocentrism of present-day discourses and institutions has proven
exceedingly difficult to displace.

Even though there has been a dearth of effective attempts to challenge and displace present-day anthropocentrism, there has been no
shortage of innovative attempts to overcome the fragmentation of the
left concomitant with the proliferation of new social movements that
I mentioned above. A whole host of post- and neo-Marxist thinkers
with a universalist bent have argued that the proliferation of political
differences and particularities does not, of itself, lead to a radical political program; they further argue that the fragmentation characteristic of
the explosion of identity politics needs to be sutured around that which
is abject, void, and excluded from the universal—but this argument is
made precisely in the name of saving *the universal*. Inasmuch as emanci-
patory politics is about the universal, it is in principle against exclusion,
and to identify with what is excluded from the universal is to struggle on
behalf of the universal and expose as false any purported universalism
that is not inclusive.

The problem with this "solution" to the proliferation of identity-
based political movements and left hegemony is that it remains, at bottom, anthropocentric. The universal and that which is abject from the
universal is almost always presented and understood in these debates as
revolving around the human. The abject here are those human beings

who have been prejudicially excluded from the realm of the universal, and the concern for the abject and the universal never extends beyond a simple and rather uncritical anthropocentrism. There is in these arguments no parallel analysis of how the universal functions (falsely) to exclude not only those human beings who are not recognized as such but also those "nonhuman" animals who are figured by and excluded from the universal.

It might be thought that the way to address this limitation is to maintain the universal, both in its political and ethical forms, in a state that is *truly and perfectly empty*—and I will indeed make this argument in subsequent chapters. But the leap from a humanist, anthropocentric (and falsely empty) universal to a truly empty, nonanthropocentric one is not to be achieved all at once. In order to understand the necessity for this transition and to appreciate the stakes involved therein, it is important first to understand how deeply anthropocentric much of our thinking about animals and other forms of nonhuman life is. It is also important to understand that the contemporary debates surrounding difference-based identity politics and universalism take place within the same anthropocentric horizon that grounds and structures the very institutions that progressive thinkers hope to transform. In the course of exploring these issues, I will suggest that the genuine critical target of progressive thought and politics today should be *anthropocentrism* as such, for it always one version or another of *the human* that falsely occupies the space of the universal and that functions to exclude what is considered nonhuman (which, of course, includes the immense majority of human beings themselves, along with all else deemed to be nonhuman) from ethical and political consideration. Posthumanist theorists have taken as their critical target the "metaphysics of subjectivity" (or selfhood), and have sought to develop a thought of politics and relation that is pre-subjective and postmetaphysical. The argument that I am making here takes off from this point in order to argue that in order for this thought to be completed, the "presubjective" site of relation must be refigured in radically nonanthropocentric terms. The subject is not just the *fundamentum inconcussum* of modernity but is the avowedly *human* locus of this foundation—and this point needs to be explicitly recognized and contested as such. Unless and until this shift in thought takes place, posthumanist thought will end up undermining its aims and becoming yet another form of anthropocentrism and subjectivism.

I have just spoken of the "metaphysics of subjectivity." The phrase is typically associated with Martin Heidegger's reading of the history of Western thought. For Heidegger the phrase "metaphysics of subjectivity" is, strictly speaking, pleonastic, inasmuch as the history of metaphysics simply *is* the unfolding of related notions of subjectivity. To be more precise, Heidegger argues that the founding, unfolding, and completion of Western metaphysics proceeds according to varying models of the human subject as present both to itself and the beings it encounters in the world. More basic than these modes of subjective and objective presence, however, is the primordial co-exposure of subject and world prior to their division into a binary opposition. Heidegger argues that metaphysics is founded upon a forgetting of originary co-exposure and the thinking that proceeds from this primordial site. Heidegger's "critique" of the subject works backward through the history of metaphysics in order to uncover traces of what has been overlooked in the founding and development of the metaphysical tradition. Derrida's critical analysis of subjectivity, with which the phrases "metaphysics of subjectivity" and "metaphysics of presence" are also typically associated, shares many of the fundamental assumptions of Heidegger's critical thoughts on the concept of subjectivity. Similar to Heidegger's position on the issue, Derrida argues the concept of subjectivity is irreducibly metaphysical and linked to presence and self-identity. For both of these thinkers, the primary task of thought is to call this notion of the subject into question in order to give thought to what the concept of the subject forecloses (whether this foreclosed alterity is understood in terms of "writing" or *Ereignis,* and so forth).

While I would question the kind of conceptual fundamentalism (where the concept of the "subject" is somehow *irreducibly* metaphysical) to which Heidegger and Derrida are both committed in their analyses of metaphysics, I would agree that the notion of the subject carries considerable metaphysical baggage and that it is founded on the forgetting of an alterity that both founds and continually disrupts subjects. Consequently, I share the general disposition of both Heidegger and Derrida in their critique of the metaphysics of subjectivity. But there are additional reasons to pursue this line of thought that are germane to the arguments being made here. Over and beyond the metaphysics of presence and self-identity concomitant with metaphysical notions of subjectivity, the concept of subjectivity is almost always presented in anthropocentric terms as well. The subject is never simply a neutral subject of experience but is almost always a *human* subject, and metaphysics is founded just as primordially, if not more so, on a meditation on specifically *human* modes of subjectivity.

In fact, it is precisely this implicit anthropocentrism that leads me to take a critical distance here from most of the current postphenomenological (for example, Levinas) and neo-Marxist and neo-Lacanian (for example, Slavoj Žižek and Alain Badiou) political theorists who seek to recover the concept of subjectivity from its critique. In both of these traditions, the so-called critique or "death" of the subject is viewed more as hyperbole than as a genuine advance in theory. Thinkers such as Žižek, Levinas, and Badiou argue that the concept of subjectivity is not fully reducible to the autonomous subject of modernity and that the trend toward abandoning subjectivity as a ground for thought is a serious mistake for the radicalization of ethics (Levinas) and politics (Žižek and Badiou). To be sure, none of these authors seeks a return to the mode of subjectivity that Heidegger, Derrida, and others in this tradition have called into question. Instead, they argue that the concept of "the subject" contains within itself the elements of an alternative understanding of subjectivity inasmuch as being a subject also means being *sub-ject,* literally thrown-under something other than itself as a support. If this valence of the concept is kept in mind, we can see that the notion of subjectivity has the potential to be used as a radical ethical and political concept. The subject in this context is no longer the autonomous, domineering, atomistic subject of modernity but becomes instead the witness to and bearer of an event that exceeds and calls the singular subject into being. The subject, when understood as one who bears and is responsible to an event and alterity that exceeds it, is far from the fully self-present and self-identical subject whose existence and death have been proclaimed in the discussions over humanism and the metaphysics of subjectivity.

And yet, even if this concept of subjectivity functions in postphenomenological and neo-Marxist and neo-Lacanian discourse as a means of opening onto something other than metaphysical *humanism,* it is not at all clear that it opens onto something other than metaphysical *anthropocentrism.* When these theorists speak of the subject as being called into being as a response to an event of some sort, it is always a *human* subject that is being described, and it is always an *anthropogenic* event that gives rise to the human subject. There are never in these texts any animal or nonhuman subjects anymore than there are subject-constituting events that proceed from nonhuman life. At best, animals and other nonhuman forms of life are figured as beings who might "intrigue and charm" us;[2] but they are never event-al subjects themselves, nor are they capable of constituting an event for which, and in response to which, a subject might come into existence.

One of the points I hope to make convincingly in this book is that this kind of implicit anthropocentrism is one of the chief blind spots of much of contemporary Continental philosophy, and that the work of thinkers like Derrida and Gilles Deleuze can be used to expose these blind spots and aid in the process of challenging and moving beyond them. One of the main debates currently being carried out in Continental philosophy concerns the possible limitations of thinkers like Derrida and Deleuze for radical politics and how their critique of subjectivity purportedly leads to a political dead end. What I want to suggest here, and will argue for in later chapters, is that the ultimate stakes of the critique of subjectivity in the work of thinkers like Deleuze and Derrida (and, to a lesser extent, Agamben) have been thoroughly misunderstood. The central issue concerning the critique of the metaphysics of subjectivity concerns more than the consequences of a certain legacy of Cartesian subjectivity in modernity and postmodernity; if this critique is understood in a rigorous manner, it leads us to see more fully the inner connection between metaphysical humanism and metaphysical anthropocentrism. To allow this anthropocentrism to go unchallenged renders thoroughly unradical and conservative much of what today goes by the name of radical politics and theory. It is essential that the signposts toward a nonanthropocentric or critically anthropocentric thought that Derrida, Deleuze, and related thinkers have opened not be shut down in the name of a hasty retrieval of anthropocentric subjectivity toward supposedly radical political ends.[3]

SUMMARY OF THE CHAPTERS

Allow me, in closing, to summarize briefly the main points of each chapter. The first chapter, "Metaphysical Anthropocentrism" looks at

Martin Heidegger's discourse on animals and animality. I argue that despite there being several promising avenues for thought opened up by Heidegger's critique of human chauvinism and metaphysical humanism, his work ultimately remains dogmatically anthropocentric. In the second chapter, "Facing the Other Animal," I examine Levinas's scattered remarks on animals and evaluate whether his thinking is compatible with a radical animal ethics and politics. I suggest that his work, when understood rigorously and when stripped of the idiosyncratic anthropocentric dogmatisms that sometimes plague it, is immensely important for opening up other ways of thinking about animals in ethical and political terms. Chapter 3, "Jamming the Anthropological Machine," has as its focus the work of Giorgio Agamben. Here I trace the formation of the question of the animal in his work in order to argue that his recent work on animals constitutes an important rupture in his thought. I focus in particular on Agamben's argument that we should abandon the human-animal distinction on both a political and ontological level and discuss the critical promise and difficulties associated with such a project. In the fourth and final chapter, "The Passion of the Animal," I turn to the work of Jacques Derrida, who, as I mentioned above, has written at length on issues involving animals. There I argue for the importance of the question of the animal for understanding his larger philosophical project and demonstrate how his work serves both to further and limit the critique of anthropocentrism advanced throughout the book.

CHAPTER ONE

Metaphysical Anthropocentrism

Heidegger

INTRODUCTION

For our task of examining the question of the animal in the context of contemporary Continental philosophy, Martin Heidegger is an essential reference and ideal point of departure. He has set the agenda for numerous areas of research in Continental thought, and his influence on contemporary phenomenological, deconstructive, and psychoanalytic approaches to philosophy is immeasurable. For issues having to do with animals, Heidegger's work contains a number of important (albeit contentious) reflections on the nature of animal life and the status of the human-animal distinction. Despite my respect for Heidegger's thought and for the originality of his thinking in so many areas of philosophical inquiry, my reading of his work in this chapter will be deeply and, at times, harshly critical. It is my contention that his work has served primarily to marginalize the animal question in contemporary thought, and I approach his work with the aim of uncovering where and how it derails the kind of approach to animal issues that I am advocating here. As critical as my reading will be, it should be evident that the questions and theses pursued in presenting my position are fundamentally indebted to the horizon of thought opened up by Heidegger. In a certain sense, one could read this chapter and each of the following chapters as an attempt to deepen and extend certain lines of Heidegger's thought while simultaneously holding open other lines of inquiry that his work brushes up against but ultimately forecloses.

Animal Being: Regrounding the Human and Zoological Sciences

I begin here with Heidegger's early texts on animals, specifically his magnum opus *Being and Time*.[1] Discussion of animals is, for the most part, conspicuously absent from this text. The being of other animals nowhere commands Heidegger's sustained attention within the context of his existential analytic of Dasein, and in those few places where animals are discussed explicitly in the text, the larger philosophical stakes of the human-animal distinction go unmentioned. Thus, for instance, we find in Heidegger's discussion of *Zuhandenheit* in part 1, chapter 3, a brief discussion of the role that animal skins play as materials that are "referred" to in the production of leather shoes. These skins are "taken from animals, which someone else has raised,"[2] as Heidegger notes (and, it should be remarked, the skins are taken from animals that someone else has *slaughtered*—a fact that Heidegger does not note). And yet, despite animals having the status of little more than mere material in the production of leather shoes in this context, Heidegger notes that animals as such do not appear phenomenologically *simply* as human-produced material for use in human products. For not only do we encounter animals in contexts completely outside the scope of human domestication (for example, in "nature"), but even when we do encounter animals that have been subjected to human domestication and reared with humans ends in mind, we seem to be encountering beings that are something *more* than human artifacts. Animals are not fully reducible to the status of human creations but rather are beings that "produce themselves."[3] However, this unique manner of animal existence is quickly set aside by Heidegger, and its implications for understanding the respective differences between human and animal modes of Being (differences that, as I shall discuss momentarily, lie at the very heart of the existential analytic of Dasein) are not pursued.

Later in *Being and Time*, in part 2, chapter 1, when Heidegger turns to a discussion of Dasein's unique mode of being-toward-death, animals reappear briefly in order to highlight a contrast between animal death and Dasein's specific modality of finitude.[4] Here Heidegger explains that, starting from the viewpoint of the life sciences, Dasein's death can be studied in precisely the same ways that one might study an animal's death. In doing so, one could analyze the cause of Dasein's death, its longevity, propagation, and so forth. But such an analysis would miss the ontological characteristics specific to human Dasein's finitude, which is to say, the unique manner in which Dasein dies (or, more strictly in Heidegger's terms, *demises*) and has its being only in relation to its finitude (a modality of finitude that Heidegger calls *dying*). Inasmuch as Dasein has a relation to death as such and to death in terms of its own finitude, it never simply *perishes* or comes to an end. By contrast, animals (as instances of the kind of beings that merely have life but have no relation to finitude) never properly die or demise; they can only perish. Demise and dying are modalities of finitude to which animals simply do not have access on Heidegger's account.

As Jacques Derrida has argued, the distinctions that Heidegger tries to maintain between human and animal modes of death in this analysis are rather dogmatic and lack sufficient scientific and ontological grounding.[5] But even acknowledging the weight of Derrida's critique, it is not at all clear that the discussion of animal modes of death or the analysis of how animals appear within the average everyday world of Dasein is intended by Heidegger to constitute a fundamental ontology of animality. Any effort to develop a fundamental ontological analysis of the Being of animals would, on Heidegger's account, be premature without first having reraised the question of the meaning of Being. Heidegger's argument in the opening sections of *Being and Time* aims to establish that the *Seinsfrage* is best pursued in view of determining the meaning of the Being of human Dasein. Whatever the merits of the argument for the ontic priority of Dasein as the focal entity in the posing of the *Seinsfrage,* it is clear that the only charitable way to read Heidegger's brief discussion of animals in *Being and Time* is as a mere fragment of a more complete ontology of life, and completion of such an ontology would be subsidiary to and contingent upon a genuine engagement with the *Seinsfrage.* Even Heidegger's extensive existential analytic of Dasein should be seen as incomplete and preparatory inasmuch as the analytic is undertaken only with the posing of the *Seinsfrage* in mind. Consequently, if one looks to *Being and Time* to uncover what Heidegger takes to be the fundamental being of animals, one can only be disappointed.

But this is not to suggest that Heidegger does not have the question of the being of animal life in view in this text. Twice in *Being and Time* Heidegger refers to the importance of the project of determining the meaning of the Being of life (which presumably includes both plant and animal forms) and argues that this project would have to take the form of a "privative interpretation," starting from the "life" of Dasein and showing how nonhuman life is "deprived" of certain aspects of Dasein's unique mode of Being. Although one could take issue with Heidegger's inclination toward a privative interpretation of animal life (and this is something I will examine in more detail shortly), it is at least clear that the animal question and the larger question of the Being of life is not outside the scope of Heidegger's thought at the time of the composition of *Being and Time*, even if the possibility of examining this question in detail is outside the scope of that particular text.

Furthermore, it is important to recall that although Heidegger's focus in *Being and Time* is primarily on the Being of human Dasein, the aim of the book is not simply to provide the ontological grounding for a philosophical anthropology or for research in the human sciences. One of the primary stakes of the book is, in fact, a revitalization of science *as such*, a revitalization that can only occur by placing science on fundamental ontological grounds. It is with this project in mind that Heidegger speaks of a productive logic of the Being of beings, a saying of beings that allows beings to manifest themselves in their Being. This sort of "productive logic" leaps ahead of the sciences, rather than "limping along" behind them and collecting and analyzing their results.[6] And it is in this context that Heidegger speaks of the crisis in the foundations of the science of biology, a science that has animal and other forms of life as its object of inquiry. Presumably, Heidegger's aim in returning to the *Seinsfrage* is to reorient biology and the other sciences along fundamental ontological lines, much as he hoped to do with the human sciences. Thus, once again we can see that despite Heidegger's anthropocentric (or, more precisely, Dasein-centric) orientation, questions concerning human *and* nonhuman life lie at the very heart of his philosophical project.

Although Heidegger never carried through on this project of developing a productive logic for the sciences that he proposed in *Being and Time*, there are a handful of texts where he takes up elements of such a project. With regard to the Being of life and animals, in particular, Heidegger offers a lengthy and intricate analysis in his lecture course of 1929 and 1930, *Fundamental Concepts of Metaphysics*.[7] Here he also addresses the complicated relationship between science and philosophy and the role philosophy might play in determining the Being of animal life—a task that is often reserved solely for the sciences. Now, if Heidegger's remarks on animal death in *Being and Time* displayed a notable failure to engage with the relevant scientific literature on animals, the same certainly cannot be said for the lecture course. What we find in this text is a deep familiarity with the biological and zoological debates of the day and an attempt to develop a more reciprocal and mutually informing relationship between the sciences and philosophy. Heidegger envisions a mature form of "communal cooperation" (*FCM*, 190) between the sciences and philosophy, where the different modes of inquiry are engaged in two aspects of the same task: investigating the Being of beings as they show themselves in and of themselves. As such, the aim of the lecture course is not to demonstrate that philosophy has privileged access to the Being of specific entities (e.g., animals) over and above science but rather to show that the philosophical task of determining the essence of animals, their animality, is something that can only be done by way of a thinking confrontation with concrete scientific research and a reorientation of scientific inquiry along those lines.

Consequently, Heidegger's remarks on animals here need to be seen against this backdrop. They derive from a certain orientation toward zoology and biology and cannot be elucidated independently of this orientation. To be specific, Heidegger here sees himself as entering the fray of a debate within the sciences over the nature of life and the proper methodological and interpretive tools for understanding it. He aligns himself with contemporary zoologists and biologists who reject the attempt to analyze life by reducing it to physics and chemistry. The other dominant approaches to understanding animal life (vitalism and variations on human psychology) are similarly rejected inasmuch as they impose categories on animal life that derive from and are appropriate to other regions of beings besides animals. Heidegger believes that the zoology and biology of his day are engaged in essential thinking inasmuch as they resist the "tyranny of physics and chemistry" (*FCM*, 188) and try to determine life autonomously and with an eye toward the way in which living beings manifest themselves on their own terms. At the same time, as the lecture course unfolds, Heidegger distances himself from these same biologists when they try to bring human beings wholly within the scope of their discipline. This so-called biologistic analysis of human beings commits the same "sin" of reductionism that he associates with the tyranny of physics and chemistry in the sciences.

Human existence cannot, on Heidegger's account, be understood in terms borrowed from biology and zoology inasmuch as animal life and human life represent two distinct and essentially different regions of beings. The aim, then, is to have a cofounding relationship between the sciences and metaphysics, where the positive researches of the sciences inform and are informed by fundamental concepts drawn from careful metaphysical and phenomenological analysis of the Being of specific regions of entities. For Heidegger, this entails not reducing one kind of being to another, on the one hand, and not conflating one kind of being with another, on the other hand. In the case of undertaking a properly biological and zoological analysis of animals, the risk for Heidegger would be either reducing animals to mechanistic entities or conflating them with human beings.

It is with this double risk in mind that Heidegger focuses upon the concept of "world" in the second portion of his lecture course. This concept allows him both to distinguish human beings (who are "world-forming") from animals (that are "poor in world") and to uncover their respective, essential modes of Being. Of course, the overarching aim here is not uncovering the animality of animals but rather trying to determine the unique relation to world characteristic of human Dasein, such that this unique relation poses a genuine question and problem for metaphysical research. As such, the lecture course is centered on human existence, not animal life. And yet, despite this anthropocentric focus, Heidegger gives serious attention to a phenomenological and metaphysical analysis of the Being of animals, and tries to do so *on the animal's own terms*. It is this orientation—that of trying to think through animal Being in nonanthropocentric terms—that constitutes the most radical aspect of the lecture course and makes Heidegger's thought an important starting point for my posing of the question of the animal in the chapters that follow. Although the results of his investigations are ambiguous and deeply problematic, Heidegger's false starts in posing the question of the animal will nevertheless be useful for providing the coordinates for my readings of Levinas, Agamben, and Derrida and for thinking through the difficulties of doing philosophy in a nonanthropocentric manner.

Heidegger initially arrives at his much-discussed theses on world (the stone is worldless, the animal is poor in world, and man is world-forming) through the anthropocentric avenues of commonsense notions and Christian ideas about the place of human beings among other "created" beings. In this commonsense and religious notion of "world," human beings are part of the world but also stand over and against it to a certain extent, and in a way that animals and nonliving beings that are fully immersed in the world cannot. Now, were Heidegger to content himself with these commonsense ideas, there would be little of interest in his analysis. What makes his discussion useful for my purposes is that he takes these dominant ideas and immediately subjects them to a thoroughgoing critical examination. Unlike much of the philosophical tradition that precedes him, Heidegger does not take it as *philosophically* evident that there is a straightforward distinction to be drawn between human being and animal, or between living beings and nonliving beings. Furthermore, he poses *as a question* the proper means of getting at the Being and world relations characteristic of nonhuman entities, which is to say, he does not take for granted the idea that our anthropocentric commonsense or even scientific approaches to understanding nonhuman beings will provide the best means of access.

In order to guard against slipping back into these dominant ways of thinking about nonhuman beings, Heidegger stresses that standard hierarchical evaluations of the human-animal distinction are highly suspect (*FCM*, 194). If, for instance, we were to follow common sense in saying that humans have a "richer" world than animals—that is to say, that humans have a broader and more complex range of experiences and entities available to them in comparison with animals—then we would miss the specificity of the relations that obtain between animals and the beings they encounter in their environments. It would be counterproductive, according to Heidegger's analysis, to undertake a comparative examination of the respective world relations of human beings and animals if one were to proceed under the seemingly obvious assumption that animals are somehow "lower" or "simpler" than human beings. Such hierarchical evaluations imply that the differences between human beings and animals can be figured in terms of differences of *degree,* differences that indicate that human beings possess a range of abilities and relations that are of a higher rank than animals.

Heidegger finds these dominant ideas about animals suspect, first of all, for the obvious reason that they are empirically false. In many ways, various species of animals have extremely complex and rich relations to other beings in their environment—relations that often equal and even surpass the complexity of human relations in certain ways (consider, for example, a bird's sense of sight or a dog's sense of smell). But he also rejects this degree-of-difference manner of making comparisons and distinctions because it presupposes that human-world relations and animal-world relations can, in fact, be compared in terms of shared similarities and dissimilarities. Strictly speaking, Heidegger's comparative examination is meant to highlight the *abyssal* differences between human and animal relations to world. There is no difference in *degree* or quantity between human and animal, Heidegger insists, but rather a difference in *kind,* and this difference in kind is meant to be understood in the most fundamental and radical way possible. The difference between the Being of human beings and that of animals marks a gap and a rupture that is utterly untraversable. In this sense, the animal's world can never be compared *with* the human world, only *to* the human world (and vice versa). In insisting on ruptures and abysses, Heidegger is also clearly seeking to distance himself from any attempt to reduce the Being of human Dasein to biological (i.e., Darwinian) terms. Whatever usefulness a Darwinian analysis of human nature might have from a scientific perspective or for scientific purposes, such an analysis would only miss the specific nature of human Dasein inasmuch as it seeks to understand human beings in terms that are drawn from animal life and the rest of the natural world. Heidegger's aim, then, is to determine the respective world relations of human beings and animals by choosing terms and a mode of access that are appropriate to each *kind* of being. In regard to animals, this would mean examining them not through ideas borrowed from common sense or through notions acquired from human psychology but rather "by taking a look at animality itself" (FCM, 195) and by finding out what being "poor in world" means on animality's own terms.

It is precisely at this juncture of the text that the most promising and provocative elements, along with the most dogmatic and problematic assumptions, of Heidegger's thought on animals emerge. The effort to examine the specific mode of Being of animals and their specific world relations *on their own terms* is, when viewed in contrast with much of the previous philosophical tradition, a remarkably progressive and important advance. All too often, animals are viewed by philosophers strictly through a human lens and found to be lacking in one or several traits or capacities that are supposedly unique to human beings.

That Heidegger is at pains throughout the lecture course to avoid this same mistake renders his text one of the more important signposts for indicating a path beyond the anthropocentric limits of the philosophical tradition. At the same time, the overarching aim of Heidegger's project—that of determining the world relations of human beings and animals by demarcating a difference in *kind* between the two groups—is itself one of the most classical and dogmatic of philosophical prejudices. Even though Heidegger initially acknowledges that "it is difficult to determine . . . the distinction between man and animal"—an acknowledgment that helps to prevent his discussion from falling back into commonsense presuppositions about the human-animal distinction—the question concerning *whether such a distinction between human beings and animals can or even should be drawn* is never raised for serious discussion.

Even if we are convinced by Heidegger that hierarchical versions of the human-animal distinction are deeply suspect, it does not follow that the distinction itself should continue to stand or that it should serve as a guide for further thought in philosophy or the sciences. If our aim is to examine the specific mode of Being of what we call "animals" on the animals' own terms, isn't one of the risks of this project that the human-animal distinction may fall by the wayside? How can we be assured at the outset of the analysis that the difference between human Dasein and animal life is definitive and *abyssal,* especially if the most refined bodies of knowledge we have from the empirical and social sciences strongly suggest otherwise? Given that one of the respective "regions" of beings—viz., animal life, which for Heidegger, would include a range of beings extending from mammals, birds, and fish through insects and single-celled beings such as amoebae (*FCM,* 186)—under discussion here includes literally billions of species, is it not rather imprudent and naïve to assume that a sharp distinction can be drawn between animals as such and human Dasein as such? From what perspective does one make such assumptions? And how does empirical research figure in the drawing of these metaphysical distinctions between human beings and animals? If, as Heidegger suggests, there should be a robust "communal cooperation" between the sciences and metaphysics in determining the fundamental concepts that guide a science, we will certainly want to know if empirical evidence confirms the distinctions and concepts he is proposing and also whether the concepts are productive in the accumulation of further empirical evidence. More important, as we look at Heidegger's text in more detail, we will have to examine carefully whether the distinction between human Dasein and animals is actually drawn from "looking at animality itself" and looking at Dasein itself, or whether the distinction is simply imposed from the outside in a dogmatic fashion.

The flip side of the risk that attends Heidegger's efforts to draw a sharp distinction between the world relations of human Dasein and animals is that animals will be seen as "merely" material, mechanistic beings, something like the Cartesian version of animal automatons. In other words, if animals, in being "poor in world," are deprived of world, how do animals differ from the "worldless" stone? Aren't the stone and animal alike in lacking world altogether? What else could the animal's being deprived of world mean? Heidegger insists that animals should not be strictly identified with material entities such as stones; reductionist-style scientific projects that do so would, on his account, miss the specific Being of animals. The world relations of the stone and the animal are, for Heidegger, completely different, as different in kind as the world relations of human and animal are. If "world" means something like the space in which beings are accessible to and dealt with by a given entity, then, according to Heidegger, the stone has no world at all. It cannot be deprived of world because it has no opening to the beings that surround it. A stone "crops up" among a whole host of other beings but has no affective or relational structure that would grant it access to those other beings. By contrast, the animal *does* have access to those beings among and with which it lives. Heidegger writes that "every animal as animal has a specific set of relationships to its sources of nourishment, its prey, its enemies, its sexual mates, and so on. These relationships, which are infinitely difficult for us to grasp and require a high degree of cautious methodological foresight on our part, have a peculiar fundamental character of their own" (FCM, 198). Consequently, the animal is fundamentally different from the stone in having a series of relationships with and access to other beings in its environment. In this sense, the animal *does* have world.

Heidegger's worry is that if we examine the animal world from this perspective and fail to note the difficulty and caution required to understand it on the animal's own terms, we will be tempted to assimilate it once again to the human relation to world and interpret the human-animal distinction in terms of a difference of degree of having-world.

Even if the animal has a relation with and access to the entities in its environment, this does not mean, Heidegger argues, that the animal and the human Dasein have the *same* relational and affective structure. In particular, no matter how rich and complex a given animal's world might be, that world never grants it access to another being *as such,* that is, to the Being of an entity. Only human Dasein is capable of relating to beings *as* beings—a tree *as* a tree, a dog *as* a dog. This "as" structure, which marks the uniquely human opening to world and Being, is something forever barred from animal life. And it is this "as" structure that the animal is deprived of, that the animal lacks, and that renders the animal poor in world.

Heidegger insists, somewhat contentiously, that this structure of lack attributed to animals is not an anthropocentric projection but rather emerges out of a careful analysis of animality itself. He arrives at this conclusion through consideration of the possibility of phenomenologically "transposing" oneself into another animal, by which he means going along with another animal in the specific manner in which it lives. The aim of transposition in this instance is not to *be* another animal but rather to go along with it in its unique mode of Being and its specific manner of relating to its environment. Heidegger suggests that much as we are always already transposed into other human Daseins (inasmuch as being-with is one of the *existentialia* of human Dasein), we are always already transposed into other animals. We think and view things, at least to some extent, from their perspective; we live in view of and alongside other animals. They form part of our world, and we form part of their world. But what kind of "world," precisely, do animals have? Heidegger uses the case of domestic animals to illustrate the different worlds of human Dasein and the animal. He writes that domestic animals

belong to the house, i.e., they serve the house in a certain sense. Yet they do not belong to the house in the way in which the roof belongs to the house as protection against storms. We keep domestic pets in the house with us, they *'live' with us.* But we do not live with them if living means: *being* in an animal kind of way. Yet we *are with* them nonetheless. But this being-with is not an *existing-with,* because a dog does not exist but merely lives. Through this being with animals we enable them to move within our world. We say that the dog is lying underneath the table or is running up the stairs and so on. Yet when we consider the dog itself—does it comport itself toward the table as table, toward the stair as stairs? All the same, it does go up the stairs with us. It feeds with us—and yet, we do not really 'feed'. It eats with us—and yet, it does not really 'eat'. Nevertheless, it is with us! A going along with . . ., a transposedness, and yet not. (FCM, 210)

The conclusion to be drawn here, from Heidegger's perspective, is that transposition into another animal is possible to some extent but is ultimately limited by the fact that the *Being* of animals is simply and fundamentally different from the Being of human Dasein—so much so that entirely different terms should be used in describing what might appear to be identical activities (human Dasein exists, the animal merely lives; human Dasein eats, the animal merely feeds; and so forth). Whereas human Dasein relates to beings in their Being, to beings *as* beings, animals simply have no "world" to speak of inasmuch as they have no access to the *Being* of beings in their environment.

But, surely, another analysis is possible. On the one hand, it is not at all clear that human Dasein is always already transposed into other animals. The choice of domestic animals as an example here is particularly problematic because it is precisely domestic animals that human beings are typically most capable of "going along with," of being-with. The Being of other, nondomesticated animal species remains, in many instances, completely shrouded in mystery, and we rely on scientists and experts who live with such animals for many years to provide us with even the slightest glimpse of what being-with these animals might entail. Consequently, the possibility and extent of transposition varies with the given "species" of animal and the individual animal under discussion. To draw any general conclusions about "animality" or the world relation of animals per se based on the example of domestic animals is, to say the least, a questionable way of proceeding. Likewise, to reverse the procedure and suggest that the example of a domestic animal is not just an example but a statement of essence concerning animality, as Heidegger does, is to beg the question at hand. There can be no guarantee at the outset of the investigation of the world relations of animals that all beings labeled "animal" share some essential relational structure; at the very least, this claim needs to be informed by careful empirical examination and be useful for further scientific investigation. Given Heidegger's remarks about the "communal cooperation" that should ideally occur between the sciences and metaphysics, we have further reason for doubting the validity of the conclusions drawn here. For what ethologist, whether in Heidegger's time or our own, would be willing to make statements about the world relations of animals *as such* when such structures have yet to be investigated empirically in most animal species? Is Heidegger drawing his conclusions about animal essence from evidence gained through a careful and charitable communal cooperation between metaphysics and the sciences? Or is he, rather, simply making dogmatic claims that derive from an anxious guarding of the propriety of human Dasein's supposedly unique relation to the Being of beings? What would motivate one to make claims about sharp distinctions, indeed abyssal differences, between two groups of beings without sufficient evidence?

Moreover, although Heidegger does acknowledge that domestic animals themselves "live" with human beings, that they transpose themselves into our lives, much more could be said about this overlapping of worlds. In what ways do certain animals adapt to and go along with human beings? And what does this adaptability and capacity for transposition say about the world relation of these animals? At the very least, the varied and complicated world relations among various animal species and individual animals should give us pause in attempting to draw any hasty conclusions about animals as such or about any differences that might be drawn between human beings and animals. Indeed, we might—for this cannot be ruled out a priori—be led upon further examination to the conclusion that the phenomenological notion of "world" cannot provide the ground for drawing any kind of meaningful or rigorous human-animal distinction at all, inasmuch as some animals appear to be quite "rich" in world formation.

Heidegger seems to recognize, or at least appreciate, the force of such questions and criticisms toward the end of his analysis of animality in the lecture course of 1929 and 1930. Not only does he admit that his discussion of the essence of animality is incomplete (inasmuch as it focuses primarily on the holistic and relational structure of the animal organism while ignoring the animal's "motility" [FCM, 265]), but he also acknowledges that the very manner in which his entire discussion has been framed is, at bottom, anthropocentric. The point here is quite simple but also symptomatic of much of philosophical discourse about animals. Heidegger's discussion of animality sets out to understand the animal's relation to world on the animal's own terms but acknowledges that this very project gains a sense and direction only from an anthropocentric perspective. This anthropocentrism takes two forms. On the one hand, Heidegger looks at the world relation of animals primarily as a means of delimiting the Being of animals as a distinct group, something that is of concern (on Heidegger's reading) only to human beings and philosophical inquiry. On the other hand, this analysis is undertaken, despite his best efforts to take the animal's perspective as a point of departure, solely in view of uncovering the essence of human Dasein and its unique relational structure. And this overarching aim of getting at Dasein's Being necessarily inflects and directs Heidegger's analysis. Of course, such anthropocentrism might be irreducible, and it could even be desirable in certain contexts. But there are more or less dogmatic ways of being anthropocentric, and each way has more or less problematic consequences, especially when considering the putative differences between human beings and animals.

The consequences of Heidegger's discourse on animals on later Continental thought have been significant, and I will be examining this heritage in the subsequent chapters at some length. But we also need to consider the effects of Heidegger's remarks on animals in his key early writings on his own later writings on animality. Heidegger's discussions of animality after *The Fundamental Concepts of Metaphysics* become increasingly questionable and dogmatic. Despite its flaws, the analysis that Heidegger began in that lecture course is remarkably progressive in certain ways. First, his resolute refusal of a hierarchical human-animal distinction goes a long way toward challenging dominant philosophical notions of animality. That Heidegger does not place less value on animals and that he challenges the standard notion that animals lead an impoverished existence when compared with human beings both help point the way toward a more critical, less anthropocentric way of thinking about animals. Second, his attempt to work through the question of animal relation and world from the animal's perspective is also helpful for turning philosophy away from its dogmatic anthropocentrism. Even though Heidegger fails to carry through on this task, his philosophical alliance with ethologists such as Jakob von Uexküll signals one way in which philosophical reflection could inform and be informed by a zoocentric ethology.

But why, precisely, does Heidegger fail in his task to determine the essence of animality from a nonanthropocentric perspective? As I just noted, it is not simply because Heidegger's analysis of animal Being is one-dimensional in its focus on world relations. Rather, it is primarily because *determining the Being of animals is never considered, in itself, a pressing task.* Nearly all of Heidegger's remarks on animals in his early work are made with an eye toward understanding what he considers to be the unique essence of human Dasein. It is *this* focus and *this* priority that forms the chief limit of Heidegger's thought, and this same limit will most heavily influence the philosophers examined in this book who work within the orbit of his thought. Consequently, if our aim is to reorient post-Heideggerian Continental thought along new lines, it will be this limit that must be called into question.

There are, of course, various ways in which one could defend Heidegger's primary focus on human Dasein and his concomitant marginalization of animals against the criticism I have just made. One could, for instance, argue that if thought *is* a thought of the event, and that if a renewal of animal ethics has its origins in such an event, then it is only by way of a recovery of one's Dasein that a rethinking of animal ethics could ever take place. As such, Heidegger's thought of human Dasein and *Ereignis* is actually the condition of possibility for the kind of thought and ethico-political practice I am arguing for in this book. Or, to put things in the briefest possible terms, the argument might be made that Heidegger's path of thought is what clears the way for a renewal of thought and practice involving animals (and other nonhuman beings), one that proceeds from the event of encountering other animals. And this kind of event of other animals is possible only in and through the appropriation of one's singular "site" of expropriation, that is, by being one's own Dasein. Heidegger's preponderant focus on human Dasein is, from this perspective, not anthropocentric, but Dasein-centric and, as such, event-centric. At stake for Heidegger is not human chauvinism but maintaining the unique ek-static, event-al structure characteristic of the Dasein within the human.[8]

What can be said of this kind of defense of Heidegger? I would suggest that even if one concedes that Heidegger is not simply a human chauvinist and could actually be read as clearing the way for a non-anthropocentric mode of thought (and I would readily concede both points), the argument does not come to an end with this concession. For the remnants of Heidegger's anthropocentrism are more subtle and much more difficult to uncover and contest than most of his defenders suspect. The problem here is not that Heidegger places a higher value on human beings than animals; he is deeply critical of this ontotheological thesis regarding animals. The problem is rather that Heidegger uncritically accepts two basic tenets of ontotheological anthropocentrism: that human beings and animals can be clearly and cleanly distinguished in their essence; and that such a distinction between human beings and animals even needs to be drawn. The first thesis about the precise content of the human-animal distinction can be contested on various grounds, and this is something to which I will return in my examination of Heidegger and of others authors in the following chapters. Heidegger's attempt to draw the distinction in terms of human ex-posure (Da-sein, ek-stasis) and his couching of this distinction in terms of "abyssal" differences between human beings and animals is one of the most problematic and questionable aspects of his writings. In the following two sections of this chapter, I will examine later writings by Heidegger where he draws and redraws the human-animal distinction over and against efforts to efface the distinction and create a kind of human-animal homogeneity. I have suggested thus far that Heidegger's earlier works, while promising in certain respects, are ultimately unsuccessful in elaborating a thought of animality that escapes or significantly challenges the ontotheological tradition. But beyond this criticism, the second thesis that guides Heidegger's thought—the thesis that a distinction between human beings and animals is needed and should be elaborated—is the more subtle aspect of his thought that ties (irreducibly, as I shall argue) his work to the ontotheological tradition. That a human-animal distinction should even be made and that it should form a kind of guideline for thought are metaphysical assumptions that guide Heidegger's discourse—and these assumptions are deeply questionable. To be sure, such assumptions govern so many discourses and institutions today that to call them into question is to face ridicule and charges of absurdity. What could be more obvious than the notion that there is a clear distinction between human beings and animals? And that this distinction is essential for contemporary and future philosophical reflection? I shall argue throughout this chapter and the rest of this book that nothing *today* is less obvious. Whether there is a salient way to draw a distinction between human beings and animals and whether this should even be a task for future philosophical thought are wide-open questions.

And it is only by working in and through the critical space opened up by this question that a genuinely nonanthropocentric thought might emerge.

BECOMING-ANIMAL

Heidegger's early writings on animals and animality reflect his larger philosophical and cultural concerns of that period, namely, developing a fundamental ontology that would serve to reground and reorient the human and biological sciences, as well as the university as a whole. The dual insistence that human beings and animals are essentially different and that there is an abyss that separates human existence from animal life is, then, but one plank in the development of a more general fundamental ontological thought of the essence of the human and what gives rise to Being in human existence. The catastrophic political events preceding, surrounding, and following Heidegger's efforts to realize this thought within the context of the university are well known, and I will not rehearse the details here.[9] What I would like to examine in this section, rather, is what happens to Heidegger's discourse on animality after this period in his philosophical and political activity. As is well known, during the period immediately following his resignation of the rectorship at the University of Freiburg, Heidegger engaged in an extended "confrontation" with the writings of Nietzsche. And he did so in view of at least two major critical theses. First, he sought to free Nietzsche from a simplistic racial and biologistic reading (a reading that he associated with a certain strain of Nazism, a strain from which Heidegger was keen to distance himself); second, he aimed to demonstrate that Nietzsche's thinking, despite its apparent iconoclasm, remained firmly within the confines of the orbit of Western metaphysical thought.

In fact, it is by making the second argument—that Nietzsche's thinking is essentially metaphysical and brings Western metaphysics to its fulfillment and conclusion—that Heidegger hopes to defend the first thesis that Nietzsche is not to be read biologically. That Nietzsche uses biological language and presents his philosophy as an affirmation and recovery of "life" over and against the decadence and nihilism of Western metaphysics and ethics is, according to Heidegger's reading, not to be taken as the ultimate stake of Nietzsche's thought. This language is to be understood as a sign system situated at the foreground of Nietzsche's philosophy, and it is only by penetrating beneath this rhetorical surface layer, Heidegger argues, that we can catch sight of Nietzsche's inner relationship to and complicity with the metaphysical tradition that precedes him.

What, then, ties Nietzsche to the metaphysical tradition on Heidegger's reading? It is in Nietzsche's concept of will to power that the link is to be found. The will to power should be read, according to Heidegger's controversial thesis, as both a quintessential and ultimate manifestation of the metaphysics of subjectivity that has determined the unfolding of the Western metaphysical tradition since its inception.[10] Within the Heideggerian interpretive framework, Nietzsche's will to power is transformed into an "absolute," domineering mode of subjectivity, one directly tied to and emanating from the human animal's "body" and "drives and affects."[11] In line with all postclassical philosophical thought, the human subject is determined by Nietzsche as being an *animal rationale*. Of course, Nietzsche differs from the philosophical tradition that precedes him inasmuch as the tradition has tended prioritize and absolutize the *rationalist* aspects of the *animal rationale*. Indeed, by arguing for the salience of the animal and bodily traits in understanding the human "subject," Nietzsche would appear to be mounting a direct challenge to the metaphysical tradition. But, according to Heidegger, despite the obvious differences between Nietzsche and his predecessors, Nietzsche thinks the "same" thought as the dominant metaphysical tradition: the human is nothing other than an *animal rationale*. His reversal of the privileging of rationality over animality does nothing to displace the tradition that precedes him but only reinforces its guiding thought and framework, placing the accent on human animality and downplaying or criticizing human rationality. It is in this sense that Nietzsche's thought marks, for Heidegger, the "end" of metaphysics rather than a pathway or passage "beyond" it. Nietzsche's reversal of the metaphysical determination of the human as *animal rationale* is simply the exhaustion of the possibilities offered by the metaphysical tradition. The reversal does not provide us an alternative understanding of the human but simply inverts the classical metaphysical definition—or so Heidegger would have us believe.

I want to suggest that Nietzsche's reversal of classically metaphysical ideas about animals is more complicated and has more critical promise than Heidegger recognizes and that this reversal is actually an important initial step in the larger project of displacing the anthropocentric bias of classical metaphysics. It is because Heidegger believes that the guiding thread of metaphysics is to be found in the determination and unfolding of a certain conception of *subjectivity* that he reads Nietzsche in the manner that he does, that is, as leading to the culmination of the metaphysical tradition. But what if the, or one of the, guiding threads of Western metaphysics is not just a specific determination of subjectivity but rather *human* subjectivity, or *anthropocentrism,* as such? If we were to read Heidegger from this angle, then his efforts to think in postmetaphysical terms would be foreclosed a priori inasmuch as he fails to *think* the anthropocentric ground of metaphysics and the concept of subjectivity that flows from out of this ground. And if we read Nietzsche from this same angle, then perhaps his concept of will to power and his reversal of metaphysical anthropocentrism and human chauvinism could be read as a direct challenge to and exit point from this tradition—and something other than a sign of the "end" of metaphysics.

We can approach this alternative reading of Nietzsche, somewhat obliquely but profitably, through Heidegger's analysis of Rilke in his lecture course of 1942 and 1943.[12] The reasons for taking this path are simply that Heidegger's remarks on Rilke constitute one of Heidegger's most substantial texts on animals and that Heidegger reads Rilke as providing a poetic version of Nietzsche's "basic position" (P, 148). This will provide the context for demonstrating the manner in which I believe Nietzsche's thought escapes the Heideggerian reading, while at the same time helping better to delimit the anthropocentrism of Heidegger's project. Furthermore, Rilke's well-known reversal of human chauvinism will allow us another means of approaching the issue of whether such a reversal is ultimately just another metaphysical gesture or instead constitutes the opening to a postanthropocentric thought of animals.

Heidegger's reading of Rilke and Nietzsche in the Parmenides lecture course occurs toward the very end of the lectures, following an extended argument concerning the development of the concept of truth from its inception in early Greek thought up through its Latinization in Christian theology and modernization in philosophers such as Descartes and Kant. Heidegger's narrative stresses the successive unfolding of various concepts of truth that conceal ever more fully the "essence" of the occurrence of truth in human judgment and speech. The name that Heidegger gives to the essence of truth is "the open," a term that recalls thought to the unconcealment of the Being of beings by way of human disclosure. The open names the "site" in which the event of Being occurs, and it is precisely this event that the Greek term for truth (*a-lētheia,* understood as un- or dis-concealment) recalls and that subsequent notions of truth leave in oblivion. The open, which is the precondition for the human word, which is in turn the precondition for human judgment, is the ground upon which philosophy comes into being. But, according to Heidegger, philosophy in the Western metaphysical tradition has proceeded without attention to its essential grounding in the open and the "dis-closive" nature of the human.

Heidegger discusses Rilke so as to distinguish this more primordial concept of the open from Rilke's notion of the open as it appears in his *Duino Elegies.* In particular, Heidegger is concerned that Rilke's reflections on the open might, because of their seeming poetic profundity, be taken as saying something important about the nature of human beings when, in fact (according to Heidegger), they miss altogether the essence of the human. So what exactly does Rilke say about the open that raises Heidegger's critical attention? It is the well-known passage that opens the eighth elegy that catches Heidegger's attention:

> With all eyes the creature sees
> the open. Only our eyes are
> reversed and placed wholly around creatures
> as traps, around their free exit.
> What *is* outside we know from the animal's
> visage alone . . .   (Rilke, cited in P, 153)

In this passage, we can immediately see two things that would be problematic for Heidegger. First, Rilke's notion of the open is equated with what "*is,*" with beings, whereas Heidegger's thought of the open is meant to distinguish Being from beings and to recall us to the conditions that enable the event of Being in human existence. Second, and of direct relevance to my discussion in this chapter, Rilke's open is reserved for the animal, the "creature," rather than the human. This notion of the open is in direct opposition to Heidegger's, which reserves the space of the open and all that emerges from this site (history, Being, language, truth, and so forth) for the human alone. Both Rilke's notion of the open and the privileging of the animal's relation to "what is" are, according to Heidegger, mere expressions of a biologistic and pscyhologistic metaphysics that is grounded on a "complete oblivion of Being" (P, 152). And it is because of this oblivion that modern metaphysics and Rilke's poetic expression of it are ignorant of "all laws of Being" (P, 152), the most basic of which concerns the inextricable relation between the unconcealment of beings and the dis-closive capacity of the human. To suggest, as Rilke does, that animals have a privileged access to "what is" is to misunderstand profoundly the relation between Being and beings, a relation that can occur and be raised for thought only through human beings who ek-sist in the open. The ultimate consequence of this confusion and reversal of the essence of human and animal, Heidegger suggests, is "an uncanny hominization of the 'creature,' i.e., the animal, and a corresponding animalization of man" (P, 152).

What Heidegger means by the "uncanny" hominization of the animal and animalization of the human can be better understood if we recall his characterization of the development of Western metaphysics as a series of determinations of human subjectivity in which the human is figured as an *animal rationale*. Rilke's privileging of the animal with regard to access to "what is" inverts the classical determination of human chauvinism that views the human animal's rationality as the unique source of knowledge of the real. In the eighth elegy, Rilke portrays rationality and human consciousness as flawed means of accessing what is. Human knowledge "mirrors" and "arranges" what is but is never able to see the open in an unmediated manner, a "capacity" that is unique to animals. It is in this sense that the ir- or a-rational animal is "superior" to the rational human animal of Western metaphysics in Rilke's elegies. The animal takes on human characteristics and gains human privilege (the animal becomes the being with privileged access to what is) while the human is placed in the position of the animal inasmuch as it has a lower rank and is forever barred from the realm of genuine knowledge of what is. This reversal of human rank and ontological and epistemological privilege in Rilke's poetry is what is uncanny according to Heidegger; for what appears to be a radical reversal of the tradition is in fact deeply indebted to and rooted in that very tradition. In other words, just as with Nietzsche, Rilke's poetry is but another symptom of the end of metaphysics rather than a postmetaphysical mode of thought.

Heidegger's contestation of Rilke's metaphysical reversal of human epistemic privilege is aimed at more than simply recovering the essence of the human in the wake of its concealment in Western metaphysics. Heidegger also believes that reversing the standard metaphysical understanding of the animal—understood as being the entity with *ratio* or *logos*—does nothing to help to *disclose the unique essence of animality*. In fact, viewing the animal as being without logos or rationality, whether this is given a positive or negative valence, does nothing to promote understanding of the specific Being of animals. Even when the traits of being "arational" or "nonspeaking" take on a positive value, as they do in Rilke and Nietzsche, these traits are still nothing more than the negation of supposedly unique human characteristics. To say that the animal *lacks* them says very little *positively* about what the animal actually is and how it differs from other entities. It is in this sense that Heidegger can say that the kind of metaphysical thought associated with Rilke and Nietzsche does not heed the "mystery" and "enigmatic character" of the animal and ends up humanizing animals and animalizing humans.

Defenders of Heidegger's approach to thinking about animality often point to this thread in his work in order to argue that Heidegger does, in fact, respect the alterity of animals and that his thought is not anthropocentric in the metaphysical sense. Similar to what I argued earlier, my response to this defense is that Heidegger's work is only of a very limited value in contesting metaphysical anthropocentrism and does not have the force his defenders seem to believe. To be sure, as Heidegger points out, it is reductive to think about animals starting from a human-centered perspective and gauging this difference in terms of which human characteristics animals either lack or have. And inasmuch as Heidegger insists on this point, his thinking marks, as it does in so many other ways, an important departure from the tradition and a significant challenge to anthropocentrism. The problem, however, is that Heidegger is unable to maintain rigorously this nonanthropocentric approach to thinking about animals. His discourse on animals constantly falls back into an anthropocentric framework, measuring animals against what he considers to be uniquely human capacities. In doing so, Heidegger hopes to highlight the essential differences between human beings and animals and to show that the comparisons that we typically make between humans and animals and the similarities we notice are not, in fact, similarities at all—at least in terms of essence.

Against the logic and approach of comparative assessments and finding similarities between humans and animals, Heidegger draws the line between human beings and animals ever more deeply. As we have seen, he goes so far as to speak of an "abyss" of essence between human beings and animals that cannot be crossed. The question for the defenders of Heidegger's approach thus becomes: How does this rhetoric of abyssal differences and sharp delimitations between human beings and animals actually contest the anthropocentric tradition? Does it not, quite simply, only take the dominant strand of the logic of anthropocentrism (i.e., the notion that human beings and animals are essentially different) and make it even more entrenched? Furthermore, how can we reconcile this rhetoric and thought of the human-animal distinction with the rigorous research and recent developments in the sciences over this issue? Are we truly to believe that Heidegger's thought of the human-animal distinction provides a more tenable and fruitful direction for scientific, philosophical, and ethico-political research in this area than that provided by the sciences? Following Heidegger's approach seems even more questionable when we realize that the standpoint of current thought on the human-animal distinction in evolutionary theory and its associated fields in the sciences and humanities is the byproduct not just of science-as-usual (in the Kuhnian sense) but of a serious engagement with the crises that have run through the biological sciences over the last century. If any science has been forced to have a thoughtful encounter with its own foundations, surely it has been the biological sciences. Perhaps science does think, after all.

There are two additional problems with Heidegger's discourse in his Parmenides lectures, the first of which concerns the ethico-political effects of the reversal of metaphysical anthropocentrism in Rilke and Nietzsche, and the second of which relates to Heidegger's ontological commitments. With regard to the first point, Heidegger's argument pays no attention to what is involved in mounting a challenge to anthropocentric thinking and the role that poetry, art, and alternative modes of thinking might play in this task. Almost all liberatory and revolutionary movements of recent times—and the movement that seeks to displace anthropocentrism *is* just such a movement—risk this initial gesture of hierarchical reversal of binary distinctions. When a group of beings, such as animals, have been consistently de- or undervalued across a substantial time span, one of the very few ways to challenge such conceptual and institutional prejudices is to grant the devalued group a higher value than the beings to which they were negatively compared. The pitfalls of such "strategic essentialism" are well known, but the value of these kinds of strategic reversals is not wholly negative. They can at least have the effect of desedimenting long-standing ideas about the undervalued and underprivileged group in question. To stick with the example of animals, Rilke's and Nietzsche's privileging of animal experience and epistemology, while romantic and untenable in many respects, does have the effect of raising for thought the possibility that we have profoundly misunderstood animal experience and have viewed animals through a reductive, neo-Cartesian lens for too long. One can only agree with Heidegger that Rilke and Nietzsche humanize animals in certain ways and that this humanization is problematic. But it is essential that one acknowledges the limitations of this kind of Rilkean and Nietzschean approach *from a genuinely nonanthropocentric perspective*. The Heideggerian critique of Rilke and Nietzsche proceeds less from a nonanthropocentric perspective and more from a deep anxiety over the crossing and blurring of boundaries between human and animal and a desire to salvage the unique essence and relational structure proper to human Dasein. Although Heidegger pays lip service to respect for the alterity of animal life, his work does not demonstrate any abiding concern to determine with any rigor the Being of animals or to analyze the ethico-political implications of a renewed understanding of animality. Animals and animality almost always appear in Heidegger's texts as foils for a positive understanding of human essence and almost never as concepts and life forms to be understood on their own terms. And it is this very approach that makes Heidegger's thought deeply problematic from the point of view of the argument being developed here.

The other untenable aspect of Heidegger's reading of Rilke (and the related thinking in Nietzsche and the biological sciences) is found in the underlying ontological commitments of Heidegger's discourse, especially his essentialism. While his essentialism is rather different from classical philosophical essentialism and the forms of essentialism at work in contemporary identity politics, he does share with these a kind of semantic and ontological realism that involves making sharp distinctions among different beings. And it is difficult to discern what evidence—phenomenological, empirical, or otherwise—he relies on in making such ontological determinations about the essence of various beings, especially in the instance of trying to distinguish between human beings and animals. As we saw in our reading of *The Fundamental Concepts of Metaphysics,* Heidegger claims to think from and in cooperation with evidence from the sciences, but there is little evidence from the sciences that would support the ontological assumptions that guide his thought.

In general, Heidegger's discourse on animality manifests less a communal cooperation with the biological sciences and more a deep anxiety about the confusion of boundaries between human and animal in contemporary scientific, literary, and philosophical culture. This anxiety is particularly evident in a footnote appended to his reading of Rilke in the Parmenides lectures. In explaining that Rilke's use of the term "creature" in the *Duino Elegies* should be understood as referring solely to nonhuman animals, Heidegger offers the following gloss and question concerning Rilke's reversal of the human-animal distinction: "For Rilke, human 'consciousness,' reason, *logos,* is precisely the limitation that makes man less potent than the animal. Are we then supposed to turn into 'animals'?" (*P,* 154 n. 1). Even if Rilke's poetic discourse on animals were meant to urge human beings toward this possibility (which is doubtful), one wonders what the problem with such a becoming-animal of the human might be? What would be lost if human beings were somehow to become "animal" and leave behind their "higher" faculties? One gets the sense that Heidegger believes that the recovery of human essence and the uniquely human capacities that emerge from this essence are things that need to be solemnly and reverently guarded. Is this not further evidence of a dogmatic anthropocentrism in Heidegger's discourse?

The obvious antidote to such reverential and anxious guarding of human propriety is Nietzsche's opening paragraph from his 1873 essay "On Truth and Lies in a Nonmoral Sense":

> In some remote corner of the universe, poured out and glittering in innumerable solar systems, there once was a star on which clever animals invented knowledge. That was the haughtiest and most mendacious minute of "world history"—yet only a minute. After nature had drawn a few breaths the star grew cold, and the clever animals had to die.
>
> One might invent such a fable and still not have illustrated sufficiently how wretched, how shadowy and flighty, how aimless and

arbitrary, the human intellect appears in nature. There have been eternities when it did not exist; and when it is done for again, nothing will have happened. For this intellect has no further mission that would lead beyond human life. It is human, rather, and only its owner and producer gives it such importance, *as if the world pivoted around it*.[13]

The critical delimitation of anthropocentrism and human chauvinism exposed here in Nietzsche, which is reminiscent of certain gestures in Rilke's poetry, has no exact equivalent in Heidegger precisely because Heidegger takes over the classical metaphysical project of uncovering and analyzing human essence as distinguished from animal life. And if the Nietzschean and Rilkean discourse on animality is read only through a Heideggerian lens, it might appear that their respective metaphysical reversals of the human-animal distinction accomplish little more than privileging irrationality over human rationality, language, and consciousness. But there is more at stake in their discourse than the Heideggerian reading allows us to see, and we can begin to grasp what is at issue only once we have abandoned, or at least held in abeyance, the Heideggerian aim of seeking the proper of the human. Beyond this perspective, thinkers such as Rilke and Nietzsche, and others who contest metaphysical anthropocentrism, can also be viewed as urging the possibility of thinking from other-than-human perspectives and modes of existence. The displacement of human privilege and critique of anthropocentrism in such thinkers is not an end in itself (as Heidegger seems to suggest) but rather serves as the opening onto a larger set of questions that concern the expansion of thought and possibilities of living for human and other-than-human beings alike.

Nietzsche gives explicit voice to such possibilities in book 5 of *The Gay Science* in a passage entitled "Our new 'infinite.'" To be sure, as this passage demonstrates, Nietzsche is critical of the possibility of actually moving wholly beyond an anthropocentric epistemological perspective and fully inhabiting an other-than-human viewpoint. He insists that we "cannot look around our own corner: it is a hopeless curiosity that wants to know what other kinds of intellects and perspectives there *might* be,"[14] which is to say that full and genuine access to whatever other-than-human perspectives there might be is forever forbidden to human beings. But this impossibility does not lead Nietzsche to conclude, in line with metaphysical anthropocentrism, that *the human perspective is the only possible perspective.* Rather, he argues that the hasty conclusion of metaphysical anthropocentrism betrays a dogmatic and immodest attitude. Nietzsche writes:

> I should think that today we are at least far from the ridiculous immodesty that would be involved in decreeing from our corner that perspectives are permitted only from this corner. Rather has the world become "infinite" for us all over again, inasmuch as we cannot reject the possibility that *it may include infinite interpretations.* Once more we are seized by a great shudder.[15]

The (shudder) Nietzsche writes of here is the result of glimpsing the abyss opened up by recognition of the perspectival character of human knowledge and the concomitant awareness of the limits and ends of anthropocentrism, both epistemologically and ontologically. Elsewhere, he argues that the ultimate ground of human nihilism stems from being unable to withstand and think through this shudder of the limits of the human and that the immodesty and "hyperbolic naïveté" of anthropocentrism is what is responsible for the collapse of values.[16] Thus, far from fulfilling the metaphysics of modern subjectivity in the concept of a domineering human will to power (as Heidegger reads Nietzsche), Nietzsche's thought seeks to mark clearly the limits of the humanist metaphysical schema. And in distinction from Heidegger, Nietzsche clearly recognizes the conjunction between humanism, anthropocentrism, and nihilism, and understands that the most promising means of contesting this network of concepts and institutions is to be achieved through an "overcoming" of the human.

That such an overcoming of the human must pass through a metaphysical reversal of human chauvinism and a "becoming-animal" of the human is a thought that has been developed at some length by Gilles Deleuze and Félix Guattari. Following Nietzsche's lead, and extending various literary and poetic discourses on animals, Deleuze and Guattari view becoming-animal as a necessary moment in the displacement of metaphysical humanism and anthropocentrism. They contrast an ontological and epistemological standpoint anchored in human subjectivity ("being-perceptible") with the multiple and varied perspectives of non- and inhuman others ("becoming-imperceptible"), and they argue that anthropocentrism is effectively challenged only in encountering and thinking from other-than-human perspectives. Like Nietzsche, Deleuze and Guattari do not believe that becoming-animal entails actually *being* an animal. Becoming-animal and challenging anthropocentrism is not a matter, as Heidegger seems to think is the case with Rilke and Nietzsche, of imitating or identifying with animals. Rather, it is a matter of being transformed by an encounter with nonhuman perspectives. Becoming-animal is thus better understood in terms of symbiosis, affect, alliance, and contagion between beings that are usually identified as distinctly "human" and "animal."

And yet, if such encounters and becomings-animal are to be truly transformational, they must proceed in such a way that animals are not approached in familiar, anthropomorphic terms. Deleuze and Guattari suggest that animals can be seen along three primary lines, the first two of which are anthropomorphic and a third that disrupts human conceptualization: first, as familiar, individual animals who "belong" to us, what they call "Oedipal animals"; second, as beings with characteristics that can be studied in order to uncover "structures" and "models," or "State animals"; and third, as "demonic" or "pack" animals caught up in a network of machinic becomings that undercut any classificatory or Oedipal schema.[17] These three different ways of approaching animals can be applied, they argue, to any animal, even those animals with which we seem to be most familiar ("even the cat, even the dog"). It is the demonic animals that interest Deleuze and Guattari inasmuch as they offer perspectives and possibilities for becoming that displace dominant modes of human subjectivity and open the human to hybrid modes of existence. Demonic animals are not anchored to any "proper" or essential site but live and move in and through transformational becomings that make propriety impossible. By entering into conjunction with such animal-becomings, human beings themselves become-animal and enter on a path or "line of flight" leading away from human subjectivity and human perspectives toward becoming-imperceptible.

But what, precisely, drives human beings to enter into these "assemblages" with demonic animals? Deleuze and Guattari speak of a "fascination" for the animal and other nonhuman perspectives that are at work in becoming-animal; for them, it is this fascination that motivates revolutionary literature and progressive discourses on animals. From this perspective, the discourses on animality we find in such thinkers as Rilke and Nietzsche (and, for Deleuze and Guattari, Franz Kafka would be an important figure to add to this list as well)[18] are not to be understood as simplistic metaphysical reversals or invitations for human beings to become "irrational." Rather, their contestation of anthropocentrism and human chauvinism and the privileging of animality should be taken as evidence of a fascination for something "outside" or other than the human and dominant perspectives (and this "outside" might well lie within human beings, for example, in an inhuman space at the very heart of what we call human). From the theoretical perspective developed by Deleuze and Guattari, authors such as Rilke and Nietzsche can be seen as signposts on the path toward a postanthropocentric and transhumanist thinking rather than, as Heidegger would have it, the mere culmination of the metaphysical tradition that precedes them.

From Metaphysical Humanism to Metaphysical Anthropocentrism

For all of his critical remarks on Rilke, Nietzsche, and other thinkers who reverse the metaphysical human-animal distinction, it is clear that Heidegger himself at least *glimpsed* the inner connection between the metaphysical tradition and anthropocentrism that is at issue here. Of course, throughout much of his work, Heidegger stressed that the essential characteristic of metaphysical thought lies in its commitment to developing a specific notion of subjecticity in the form of human subjectivity—not anthropocentrism. But it was not altogether lost on Heidegger that the project of unfolding a specific notion of human subjectivity is, in fact, a matter of focusing on specifically *human* subjectivity. When the foundation of metaphysics is located by Heidegger in the establishment of a certain conception of truth, being, and subjectivity in Plato, he is aware that this movement is also a simultaneous establishment of anthropocentrism. Thus, with Socrates and Plato, what occurs is not just a shift in the essence of truth; there is also a shift in the ground of philosophy as such toward a locus that is unabashedly anthropocentric.

This coincidence between the establishment of metaphysics and anthropocentrism is noted by Heidegger most explicitly in his essay "Plato's Doctrine of Truth." There he suggests that the "beginning of metaphysics in the thought of Plato is at the same time the beginning of 'humanism.'"[19] In contrast with his analysis of humanism in the

"Letter on 'Humanism'" (which I will take up at length below), in "Plato's Doctrine of Truth" Heidegger understands humanism broadly to involve both the establishment of human subjectivity *and* a more general anthropocentrism. We are told that the coestablishment of metaphysics and humanism in Plato and its development in subsequent philosophy is a process that moves the human "into a central place among beings,"[20] and that what is at stake in this metaphysical project is to take human beings and lead them to their destiny through the shaping of their moral behavior, reason, civic sense, and so on. Although the accent is placed on different aspects of this project depending on which version of humanism is under discussion (Roman, Christian, Marxist, existentialist, and so on), this much remains the same in all humanisms: in each instance there is a "metaphysically determined revolving around the human being, whether in narrower or wider orbits."[21]

It might be thought, then, that Heidegger's subsequent critical engagement with metaphysical humanism would require a thorough sorting through of anthropocentrism and its effects. But Heidegger's most extended treatment of metaphysical humanism, his much-discussed "Letter on 'Humanism,'" seems to abandon the critical analysis of anthropocentrism altogether—or so I shall argue in what follows.

As those readers familiar with the "Letter on 'Humanism'" will recall, Heidegger traces the concept of *humanitas* back to the age of the Roman Republic, in which *homo humanus* was opposed to *homo barbarus.* He tells us that *homo humanus* is the name given to Romans who embodied the *paideia* of the Greeks of the Hellenistic age. *Humanitas,* the Roman translation of the Greek *paideia,* came to mean scholarship and training in good conduct. Now, subsequent versions of humanism (from Renaissance humanism, to eighteenth-century German humanism, to the versions we find in Marx and, more recently, in Sartre) differ significantly in the respective modes in which they actualize this *humanitas,* but there is, in fact, a common core to all manifestations of humanism on Heidegger's reading. Whereas in "Plato's Doctrine of Truth," Heidegger sought to link all humanisms through reference to their "metaphysically determined revolving around the human being," here in the "Letter" he suggests that a certain determination of Being as such is at the core of humanism. Thus, humanism in the "Letter" is seen as an effort to define "man" in view of "an already established interpretation of nature, history, world, and the ground of world, that is of beings as a whole."[22]

For Heidegger, it is this preestablished interpretation of the Being of beings as a whole that typifies all previous humanisms as being *metaphysical*. And it is in posing the question of the truth of Being (which is to say, the question of the conditions that allow for Being to manifest itself) to both metaphysics and humanism simultaneously that Heidegger aims to disclose their common ground. Gone in the "Letter," then, is the specific and explicit reference in "Plato's Doctrine of Truth" to the anthropocentrism of the metaphysical tradition. As we shall see, this setting aside of the question of anthropocentrism leads to dogmatism.

The operative interpretation of the Being of the human presupposed by classical humanism is, as we saw in the Parmenides lecture course, that the human being is an *animal rationale*. Heidegger finds this determination questionable in several respects. To begin with, *animal rationale* is not simply a translation of the Greek definition of man, *zōon logon echon* (the animal having discourse or language), but a *metaphysical interpretation* of this definition in which *ratio* is problematically substituted for *logos*. According to Heidegger, not only do *ratio* and *logos* denote two distinct "capacities", but the names themselves spring from a radically different relation to the Being of beings. By contrast with the Greek *logos*, the various definitions of *ratio* (as reason, a faculty of principles or categories, and so on) already presuppose and arise from within a certain preestablished interpretation of the Being of beings, thereby covering over the question of the truth of Being, that is, the question of how Being *is given* to the human and the essential cobelonging of Being and human beings. The same goes for the *animal* of the Latin *animal rationale*, which, according to Heidegger, is always interpreted by humanism in terms of a predetermined conception of the Being of animality. When Heidegger criticizes humanism for being metaphysical in the "Letter," it is these two dogmatic limits and their common ground that are being addressed.

But beyond this delimitation of the common ground of humanism and metaphysics, there is something else at stake here to which Heidegger will devote a considerable amount of effort in the remainder of the "Letter." It involves a contestation of the confusion of *humanitas* with *animalitas* in the definition of the human as *animal rationale*. Heidegger's point here is that not only is metaphysics guilty of failing to raise the question of Being regarding *ratio* and *animalitas*, it is also at fault for thinking man more on the basis of *animalitas* than his *humanitas*.

He wonders if this is the most effective means of uncovering what is essential to man: "it finally remains to ask whether the essence of the human being primordially and most decisively lies in the dimension of *animalitas* at all" (*LH,* 246). Should the human be thought of in terms of life, as one "living being" among others, among "plants, beasts, and God," as Heidegger phrases it? This is how biologism proceeds, and in so doing, it will of course be able to state important things about human beings. Ultimately, however, the biologistic approach fails to uncover the *essence* of the human—and this is why Heidegger takes his distance from biologism. According to Heidegger, when man is placed alongside other living beings, we "abandon" man's essence to the realm of *animalitas.* This occurs even if (as is the case with metaphysical humanism) man is considered different from the animal on the basis of some essential attribute, for example, having a spirit or soul, or being capable of subjectivity or personhood. An analysis of man that starts from the realm of *animalitas* and then locates the human being's essential difference from the animal by tacking on a soul or mind still falls short of thinking man's *humanitas* (*LH,* 246–7).

As Derrida recalls in "The Ends of Man," what Heidegger finds missing in this approach to man is his proper *essence* and *dignity.*[23] Man's essence lies in his ek-sistence, and it is in ek-sisting that man finds his dignity and propriety. But Heidegger is not just trying to restore man's essence and revalorize his dignity; he is doing so within the context of trying to separate decisively the essence of man from the essence of other "living creatures," especially the animal. In the "Letter," Heidegger insists not once or twice but three times that ek-sistence is not only man's proper, but his proper *alone.* He writes: "Such standing in the clearing of being I call the ek-sistence of human beings. This way of being is proper only to the human being" (*LH,* 247). And one sentence later, Heidegger asserts two more times that *only* human beings are characterized by ek-sistence: "Ek-sistence can be said only of the essence of the human being, that is, only of the human way 'to be'. For as far as our experience shows, only the human being is [*der Mensch allein ist*] admitted to the destiny of ek-sistence" (*LH,* 247). Why the insistence of and on the human? Does Heidegger merely wish to drive home the point that metaphysics has time and again overlooked man's essence as ek-sistence? Certainly, but that is not the only reason. He is also working to separate decisively human propriety from that which does not belong properly or essentially to the human. And, for Heidegger, what does *not* belong properly to man's essence is *animalitas*. The metaphysical definition of man as *animal rationale* has allowed this essential distinction to become blurred, and this is another reason why it comes under criticism in the "Letter." Thus, Heidegger's restoration of man's essence and dignity is, I would suggest, as much a matter of bringing man back into a thinking relation with Being as it is of driving a wedge between the essence of man and the essence of the animal based on this relation.

This suggestion receives further support when Heidegger turns to a discussion of embodiment (*LH,* 247 ff.). Heidegger argues here that the human body, in its essence, must be viewed as something other than the body of a living organism. He insists on this point because it is human bodies (which in many ways are so similar to other living being's bodies—especially animal bodies) that encourage us to understand man's Being in terms of *animalitas.* According to Heidegger, however, the human body and the animal body, despite certain anatomical and physiological similarities, are different in essence: "The human body is something essentially other [*wesentlich anderes*] than an animal organism" (*LH,* 247). That physiology can study the human body as an animal organism and even give us a number of interesting and useful facts in the process is, for Heidegger, no guarantee that the *essence* of the human being has been properly explained. For this to come about, the human body needs to be examined in light of its grounding in man's ek-sistence. Man's bodily interaction with other entities around him is, according to Heidegger, *essentially different* from the way nonhuman embodied beings relate to other entities, since man moves about in a "world" that grants him access to beings in their Being. Because what is essential to man is ek-sistence, that is, because he stands-out in the clearing of Being, the human body can be understood properly starting only from this essential—and essentially human—ground.

Now, in using the term "ek-sistence" to highlight the *ecstatic* element of Dasein's Being, Heidegger seeks as well as to avoid the metaphysical baggage that accompanies the concept of *existentia,* which signifies actuality in contrast to possibility, *essentia.* Using the term ek-sistence, Heidegger thus establishes a certain distance between himself and the various metaphysical interpretations of *existentia* offered by medieval philosophers, Kant, Hegel, and Nietzsche, all of whom fail to characterize accurately man's Being. Heidegger leaves it an open question whether the Being of beings other than the human is adequately conveyed with the concept of *existentia*. What Heidegger *is* able to determine with apparent certainty is that unlike human beings, living creatures (his examples are plants and animals, the stone being his example of a nonliving being) *do not ek-sist*. It is at this point that we can begin to see more clearly the stakes involved in the "Letter." If ek-sistence is proper to the human alone, then it follows that no being other than the human can have a share in it, *especially* those beings we suspect of being the most akin to us. Heidegger's essentialist logic seeks to make clean, decisive cuts where the possibility of contamination creeps in:

> Living creatures are as they are without standing outside of their being as such and within the truth of being, preserving in such standing the essential nature of their being. Of all the beings that are, presumably the most difficult to think about are living creatures [*Lebe-wesen*], because on the one hand they are in a certain way most closely akin to us [Heidegger will speak a few lines later on of our "abysmal bodily kinship with the beast"], and on the other they are at the same time separated from our ek-sistent essence by an abyss. (*LH*, 248)

Ultimately, then, not only are "living creatures" different from "us," they are different in their essence, so essentially different that a gulf opens up wide enough to be labeled an "abyss." This is not the only time Heidegger will insist on an abyss between ek-sistent man and creatures that merely live.[24] But why employ this hyperbolic rhetoric of abysses and essential differences?

On the surface of the text, it is clear that at the very least Heidegger wants to distance his own project from the determination of the Being of man made by previous metaphysical humanisms. The definition of man as *animal rationale* that humanism takes for granted is not altogether false, but it remains metaphysical. Heidegger thus opposes this metaphysical humanism in order to think man on a nonmetaphysical basis, in terms of the question of the truth of Being. This opposition to humanism does not come down then to merely advocating some form of antihumanism but rather is intended to bring about a *more rigorous humanism*, what could be called (following David Krell) a "hyperhumanism":

The highest determinations of the essence of the human being in humanism still do not realize the proper dignity of the human being. To that extent the thinking in *Being and Time* is against humanism. But this opposition does not mean that such thinking aligns itself against the humane and advocates the inhuman, that it promotes the inhumane and deprecates the dignity of the human being. Humanism is opposed because it does not set the *humanitas* of the human being high enough. (*LH,* 251)

It should be noted, though, that Heidegger goes on to argue that man's *humanitas,* his unique relation to the saying and truth of Being, should not be mistaken for a kind of mastery or tyranny over Being in which man deigns "to release the beingness of beings into an all too loudly glorified 'objectivity'" (*LH,* 252). Instead, the recovery of man's *humanitas* is meant to recall the essential finitude of the human being, man's being-thrown by Being into the truth of Being so that he may guard and shepherd it.

Thus, despite being a hyperhumanism of sorts, Heidegger's idea of humanism, inasmuch as it is grounded on the finitude of the human and its expropriation by Being, does not appear to be an anthropocentrism in any simple sense. Now, if what were at issue here were only these decentering aspects of Heidegger's work, I could subscribe to his critique of metaphysical humanism almost without reserve. But when he offers his own *determination* of man's proper mode of existence, any adherence to his path of thought must be circumscribed and subsequently brought into question. Even the most minimal determination of propriety presupposes delimitation and cutting, and even when the determination is as equivocal and indeterminate as Heidegger's "man's essence is ek-sistence," where propriety and impropriety are intertwined in such a way that neither can be said to dominate, we nevertheless need to remain vigilant about what kinds of lines are being drawn. Of course, Heidegger's nonmetaphysical definition of man appears to be so broad as to pose no concerns about exclusion. Ek-sistence is not parceled out unequally along any of the traditional lines that have separated one group of human beings from another (gender, race, class, etc.); it finds its place anterior to such distinctions. But it does *institute and is itself instituted along* a questionable dividing line separating man from animal. Reading Heidegger's thought from the perspective of the question of the animal enables us to uncover this oppositional line and to track the axioms that underlie Heidegger's rhetoric of abysses and essential differences.

Pursuing this thought further, we find that the dividing line between animal and human reappears in Heidegger's "Letter" when he shifts to an analysis of language. When Heidegger calls into question the metaphysical definition of man as *animal rationale,* he is, of course, doing so with an eye toward the more primordial Greek understanding of man as *zōon logon echon*, the animal having language. By interpreting the logos as *ratio*, metaphysical humanism misses the essential role that language plays in being-human. As I mentioned earlier, this is why for Heidegger *animal rationale* is not simply a translation of *zōon logon echon* but a *metaphysical* interpretation of it, one in which a groundless experience of *ratio* is substituted for a more primordial experience of the word. But a simple return to the Greek definition of man will not suffice either, since in labeling man "the animal having language" we run the risk of understanding language as something that arises out of, or is added on to, man's animal existence. To understand man's proper relation to language, Heidegger argues that we must begin from man's *humanitas* and not his animal nature, since animals, strictly speaking, do not have language.

Animals lack man's specific relation to language, according to Heidegger, because they lack "world." World here does not simply mean "nature" or the "environment" but signifies instead the place in which the Being of beings comes to unconcealment. "World" thus understood presupposes the capacity for ek-sistence, for standing in the clearing of Being where Being comes into presence and departs, a possibility reserved for man alone. Plants and animals do not *ek-sist* outside of themselves in the clearing of Being, but simply *live* within their surrounding environments: "Because plants and animals are lodged in their respective environments but are never placed freely into the clearing of being which alone is 'world,' they lack language" (*LH,* 248). We should not infer from this passage that Heidegger is arguing that plants and animals have no access to beings beyond themselves. As is clear from *Fundamental Concepts of Metaphysics,* Heidegger does believe that plants and animals have access to other beings around them; he denies, however, that plants or animals are able to access these other entities *in their Being,* or *as such,* in the way that human beings with language and world are able to do. Without language, which simultaneously distances man from his surrounding environment and brings him into proximity with Being, plants and animals remain lodged in their environments and continue "merely" to live without access to the Being of other beings or their own Being.

The metaphysical-animal explanation of man's essence thus covers over the close relation between being and language posited here, much as it misses man's ek-sistent essence. For Heidegger, the essence of language needs to be understood as the "clearing-concealing advent of being itself" (LH, 249), or, as he says later in the text, the bringing near of being "occurs [west] essentially as language itself" (LH, 253). This conception of language finds its contrast in the traditional conception of language as a unity of body (a phoneme or written character), soul (melody and rhythm), and spirit (meaning). The definition of man as *animal rationale* corresponds to this traditional understanding of language insofar as man's constitution is read in terms of body, soul, and spirit. Man's body in this account is what belongs to the realm of *animalitas,* and his capacity for language and reason are the specific marks of his *humanitas.* The definition of man's essence as *animal rationale* thus sets man apart as the single and sole living creature with the capacity for language. Heidegger insists, however, that language cannot be understood as arising from man's animal nature; language is not just something added on to man's essence in order to distinguish him from other living creatures: "the human being is not only a living creature [*nicht nur ein Lebewesen*] who possesses language along with other capacities. Rather, language is the house of being in which the human being ek-sists by dwelling, in that he belongs to the truth of being, guarding it" (LH, 254).

As this passage illustrates, Heidegger's contestation of the metaphysical definition of man as *animal rationale* is indeed undertaken in order to restore the privilege of being as the matter of thought, but this privilege cannot be separated from an essentialist logic that functions on another level—a logic that grants man, and *man alone,* a certain dignity in his expropriated proximity to being. It is from this perspective that we can appreciate the implications of Derrida's statement that "man and the name of man are not displaced in the question of being such as it is put to metaphysics."[25] Heidegger's thought of the truth of Being *is* a displacement of *metaphysical* humanism, but one that occurs in the name of a more exacting and rigorous determination of the human.

But—as you no doubt have been wanting to rejoin for quite a while now—does not such thinking think precisely the *humanitas* of *homo humanus?* Does it not think *humanitas* in a decisive sense, as no meta-physics has thought it or can think it? Is this not a "humanism" in the extreme sense? Certainly. It is a humanism that thinks the humanity of the human being from nearness to being. But at the same time it is a humanism in which not the human being but the human being's historical essence is at stake in its provenance from the truth of being. But then does not the ek-sistence of the human being also stand or fall in this game of stakes? Indeed it does. *(LH, 261)*

Let me, then, sum up the issue with Heidegger as clearly as pos-sible. Where classical humanisms have been content to determine man's Being in light of a presupposed determination of nature and human-ity, Heidegger has boldly raised the question of the ground of these de-terminations, thereby exposing humanism's complicity with dogmatic metaphysics and offering a new determination of man's essence as ek-sistence. With this critique of humanism and conception of ek-sistence we are given not only the possibility for a clearer understanding of the collapse of value theory and its attendant nihilism but also the possi-bility for an alternative "ethics," another thought of *responsibility itself,* of responsibility *qua* responsivity or exposure.[26] This is Heidegger's great contribution to contemporary thought and one with which I am largely sympathetic.

The problem arises, though, when Heidegger limits ek-sistence to man alone. And the issue here is not simply that Heidegger offers no analysis or argumentation in support of this claim (although this defi-ciency does pose certain difficulties); nor is the problem that this claim about ek-sistence is anything but certain. (Is anyone certain, including Heidegger himself, that ek-sistence cannot be found beyond the human? If he is certain and the case is so obvious, what is the status of his con-stant denegations and disavowals of animal ek-sistence?) The problem lies instead with Heidegger's uncritical reliance on a logic of opposition in differentiating human beings from animals. Why does Heidegger re-peatedly insist that man alone ek-sists? Could one not just as easily speak of ek-sistence *without* drawing single, insuperable lines between human and animal? Of course a less anthropocentric and more nuanced discus-sion of ek-sistence might still eventually give rise to certain distinctions and boundaries—but would these differences necessarily be essential, simple, oppositional, binary, and abyssal, and would they necessarily fall along a line dividing human from animal?

Ultimately, despite his profound analysis of the limits of metaphysical humanism, Heidegger offers nothing in the way of critique concerning the metaphysical tradition's *drawing* of the oppositional line between human beings and animals; his final concern, rather, is with the way in which this oppositional line has been *determined* and understood. Heidegger thus says the "Same" as the humanist tradition—he too insists on an oppositional logic separating human from animal. The difference in Heidegger's repetition of the Same lies in his shifting of the opposition between human and animal onto another register. The essential difference between human and animal for Heidegger lies not merely in having language or reason but in the *ground* of these capacities: ek-sistence, which is reserved for the human alone. Thus, what we find in Heidegger's text when read from the perspective of the question of the animal is an effective challenge to metaphysical *humanism* (where man is determined according to a preestablished interpretation of the Being of beings) but, at the same time, a further sedimentation and reinforcement of the *anthropocentrism* of this same humanist tradition (in which the animal's Being is determined in strict binary opposition to and against the measure of the Being of the human). Anthropocentrism is not simply a matter of placing the human being in the center of beings (something Heidegger is keen to avoid); it is also the desire to determine human specificity over and against those beings who/that threaten to undermine that specificity. It is this problematic anthropocentric remnant that Heidegger has bequeathed to contemporary thought. In the following chapters, I will track this remnant of anthropocentrism as it gets taken up, refined, interrogated, and refigured in Levinas, Agamben, and Derrida.

CHAPTER TWO

Facing the Other Animal

Levinas

INTRODUCTION

The question that guides this chapter can be stated succinctly as follows: What today remains of Levinas's thought for animal ethics? This is an important question to pose, for Levinas's thought would appear at first blush to be opposed to the main positions developed in this book. The two dominant theses in Levinas's writings concerning animals are: no nonhuman animal is capable of a genuine ethical response to the Other; and nonhuman animals are not the kinds of beings that elicit an ethical response in human beings—which is to say, the Other is always and only the *human* Other. My aim here is to examine these claims as they appear in certain of Levinas's texts and to argue that although Levinas himself is for the most part unabashedly and dogmatically anthropocentric, the underlying logic of his thought permits no such anthropocentrism. When read rigorously, the logic of Levinas's account of ethics does not allow for either of those two claims. In fact, as I shall argue, Levinas's ethical philosophy is, or at least should be, committed to a notion of *universal ethical consideration,* that is, an agnostic form of ethical consideration that has no a priori constraints or boundaries. This radical notion of ethical consideration anticipates certain of the themes to be developed in the chapter on Jacques Derrida and also helps to frame the political dimensions of the question of the animal as I present it in the next chapter, on Giorgio Agamben.

What, then, of the first claim that Levinas makes, that animals are incapable of a genuine ethical response to the Other? In order for a given animal to be capable of responding to an Other, an animal would, according to Levinas's account, have to be able to overcome or suspend its basic biological drives. Levinas holds a classical (which is to say, Hobbesian and quasi-Spinozist) view of animals as being engaged in an unremitting struggle of all against all, persisting in their egoist desires, blind and deaf to the call of the Other. For an animal to be able to suspend its basic biological drives would be miraculous on this account and completely inexplicable within the order of biology. The *human* animal is also, according to Levinas, largely determined by these same biological drives, and it, too, lives primarily by pursuing "analytically, or animally"[1] its own struggle for existence. It is only by breaking with this biological order of being that ethics and "the human" arise. Thus, the human and ethics are something like miracles in Levinas's philosophy. They mark a rupture in the order of being and point toward the "otherwise than being," which could just as easily be rewritten as the "otherwise than animality." In a certain sense, then, Levinas's entire philosophy is oriented around precisely this question: Where does the human animal break with animality and become properly human?

Of course, the opposite possibility, that the nonhuman animal could become ethical and thus properly "human" can never be completely ruled out. Instances of certain individual animals sacrificing their own well-being for members of their own and other species are legion; and while evidence for many of these occurrences is often anecdotal, sufficient numbers have been witnessed firsthand by scientists or captured on film to constitute genuine verification of radical altruism among nonhuman animals. (Indeed, as we shall see, one of the great puzzles for evolutionary biologists is why such altruism exists at all in both the human and animal world; whatever answer is given to this "puzzle," it is taken for granted by biologists and ethologists that altruism occurs quite frequently throughout nature.) Such evidence would seem, at the very least, to complicate Levinas's thesis about animal life being engaged "analytically"—that is, necessarily and naturally—in a selfish struggle of all against all. If animals are also capable of being-for-the-Other, then the chief dividing line between the human and the animal threatens to vanish in Levinas's discourse.

Curiously, Levinas himself seems to flirt with just this possibility concerning animals when reflecting on Bobby, a dog whom he encountered while a prisoner of war during World War II. Rather than paraphrasing the encounter, it is best to let Levinas describe it in his own inimitable manner:

> There were seventy of us in a forestry commando unit for Jewish prisoners of war in Nazi Germany. An extraordinary coincidence was the fact that the camp bore the number 1492, the year of the expulsion of the Jews from Spain under the Catholic Ferdinand V. The French uniform still protected us from Hitlerian violence. But the other men, called free, who had dealings with us or gave us work or orders or even a smile—and the children and women who passed by and sometimes raised their eyes—stripped us of our human skin. We were subhuman, a gang of apes. A small inner murmur, the strength and wretchedness of persecuted people, reminded us of our essence as thinking creatures, but we were no longer part of the world. Our comings and goings, our sorrow and laughter, illnesses and distractions, the work of our hands and the anguish of our eyes, the letters we received from France and those accepted for our families—all that passed in parenthesis. We were beings entrapped in their species; despite all their vocabulary, beings without language. Racism is not a biological concept; anti-Semitism is the archetype of all internment. Social aggression, itself, merely imitates this model. It shuts people away in a class, deprives them of expression and condemns them to being "signifiers without a signified" and from there to violence and fighting. How can we deliver a message about our humanity which, from behind the bars of quotation marks, will come across as anything other than monkey talk?

> And then, about halfway through our long captivity, for a few short weeks, before the sentinels chased him away, a wandering dog entered our lives. One day he came to meet this rabble as we returned under guard from work. He survived in some wild patch in the region of the camp. But we called him Bobby, an exotic name, as one does with a cherished dog. He would appear at morning assembly and was wait-

ing for us as we returned, jumping up and down and barking in de-
light. For him, there was no doubt that we were men.[2]

Among the several things that might be highlighted in this remarkable passage (which is certainly one of the most personal and moving in
all of Levinas's writings), I will focus primarily on Levinas's reference to
Bobby and how it affects the question of altruism. At first glance, Bobby's
actions (his waiting for the prisoners, his excited and delightful welcoming of their return) would not appear to constitute radical altruism per se,
but they do seem nevertheless to enact something of an ethical gesture.
Dogs are often celebrated for their capacity to respond to beings in need,
whether in regard to other dogs, human beings, or members of other
species. And Bobby's response to the prisoners—prisoners who were
treated by fellow human beings as "rabble," "subhuman beings," a "gang of
apes"—is precisely what they needed: a reminder of their humanity, that
is, of their singularity and existence beyond the figurative and literal in-
ternment into which they were forced. In recognizing and respecting the
prisoners' humanity, Bobby establishes himself in Levinas's eyes as "more
human" than the Nazi soldiers guarding the camp. This leads Levinas to refer, famously, to Bobby as "the last Kantian in Nazi Germany"
(DF, 153).
Levinas is quick to add, however, that Bobby lacks "the brain needed
to universalize maxims"—so Bobby is not, after all, properly Kantian or
human. There is a proto-ethical moment in his gestures, but no ethics
or politics proper, and thus no humanity proper. At most, animals like
Bobby are for Levinas mute and unthinking witnesses to the transcendence of the human. "Man's best friend" testifies to the freedom and
singularity of the human, and it is through this testimony that there is a
"transcendence in the animal" (DF, 152). But Levinas is perhaps missing
the more obvious point here: Bobby's life is also at stake in the camp. He is not a
pampered, Oedipal pet, but a nomad struggling to survive, living on "in
some wild patch" of the prison. He is apparently not welcome outside
or inside the camp, and is ultimately "chased away" by the guards. So
why would this dog, struggling for its very survival, break with its "persistence in being" in order to welcome the prisoners—who themselves,
tired and destitute, presumably have nothing much to give him—upon
returning from their work? Is this not the ethical act par excellence?
Admittedly, Bobby is not in a position to give anything "material" to

Levinas and the other prisoners. Bobby is not a species of the egoist "I" discussed in *Totality and Infinity,* an "I" who manages to establish a home and gather together the resources to live comfortably in the world. Consequently, Bobby cannot give any possessions "with both hands," or paws as the case may be. And yet, despite Bobby's poverty, there is an ethical gift of sorts exchanged between him and the prisoners, even if it takes a form not often noticed by Levinas. Bobby does not literally tear the bread from his mouth and give it to the prisoners, but he does pause in his struggle for existence to *be with* the prisoners and to offer them what he can: his vitality, excitement, and affection. Is not Bobby, then, a prime example of the "otherwise than being"? Are we not justified in concluding that there is a genuine transcendence *in the animal itself,* and not just in the form of a testimony to the human? Perhaps animals, too, are a miracle and mark a rupture in the order of being.

Rather than drawing this (neoreligious) conclusion, I want to argue for a complete shift in the terms of the debate. That human beings engage in acts of radical altruism is no more of a "miracle" or a rupture in the order of being than when animals do the same thing (and it is clear that they do and do so frequently). Being-for-the-Other and "holiness" among human beings and animals are not traces of transcendence but are acts that are purely and wholly immanent to the material world. Thus, rather than viewing "holiness" as the nodal point for a recuperation of postmetaphysical theology (as many of Levinas's contemporary followers do), I want to suggest that these same terms can be couched in a more expansive, fully naturalistic perspective on human and nonhuman existence. In order to pursue this thought, we need first to examine Levinas's view of animal life in more detail.

What I referred to above as Levinas's "classical" view of animals, a view I suggested was similar to the ones offered by Hobbes and Spinoza, is credited by Levinas himself to Charles Darwin. Levinas's offers the following gloss on Darwin's account of being and animality in "The Paradox of Morality":

> A being is something that is attached to being, to its own being. That is Darwin's idea. The being of animals is a struggle for life. A struggle of life without ethics. It is a question of might. Heidegger says at the beginning of *Being and Time* that *Dasein* is a being concerned for this being itself. That's Darwin's idea: the living being struggles for life.[3]

The idea that the "being" of natural entities is constituted primarily in terms of a struggle for existence is, of course, a central tenet of Darwin's theory of natural selection. But Darwin does not go as far as Levinas in claiming that being in general or animal existence in particular is *solely* a "struggle for life without ethics." On the contrary, Darwin insists that basic forms of ethical behavior can be found throughout both human society and the animal kingdom. And this should come as no surprise to anyone who has read him with some care. Perhaps no modern thinker has done more to call human chauvinism into question than has Darwin. Throughout his mature works, he remains uncompromising in his stance that the chief characteristics of human beings—including the so-called higher-order traits such as rationality, language, and morality—are not unique to human beings. Consequently, when we see rational or ethical behavior among human beings, Darwin would remind us that we will likely find versions of such behavior elsewhere in nature. Rather than a fundamental difference in kind between human beings and animals, we will instead find, he argues, only differences in degree.

Darwin is especially keen to underscore this point with regard to animal ethics in *The Descent of Man.* Against the prevailing dogma of the day (which still remains firmly entrenched in much of contemporary scientific and popular consciousness) that animals have no moral sense, he provides multiple examples of altruism and sociability in a wide variety of animal species, arguing that animals exhibit mutual affection, provide services for one another, care for kin and siblings, alert one another to danger, and even protect and provide for their injured or invalid fellows. While Darwin attributes these kinds of ethical actions to the "social instincts" that animals have in common with human beings, he has no doubt that such actions are genuinely ethical inasmuch as they proceed from strong emotional bonds among and between individual animals. Darwin himself had considerable difficulty trying to square such instances of altruism with his theory of natural selection, but it is beyond doubt that he believed that ethics exists well beyond the human.[4]

There is, however, a more recent line of neo-Darwinian thinking associated with Richard Dawkins that comes quite close to certain elements of Levinas's thinking and that would appear to provide some scientific support for his views on the fundamentally nonethical existence of animals. In his book *The Selfish Gene,* Dawkins cites several of his own examples of animal altruism and, like Darwin, believes altruism as such to be fundamentally at odds with natural selection. Dawkins argues that with regard to understanding the basic functioning of natural selection, selfishness is the only game in town: "I think 'nature red in tooth and claw' sums up our modern understanding of natural selection admirably."[5] So, how best to explain the anomalous fact that a blind and ruthlessly selfish biological system can give rise to what can only be described as acts of self-sacrifice and altruism? Biologists prior to Dawkins had given a wide range of evolutionary explanations of altruism, including kin-, species-, and other group-selectionist accounts. Dawkins sets himself sharply against these kinds of explanations and, following the groundbreaking work of Bill Hamilton and George Williams, insists that altruism can best be explained, or rather *explained away,* from a gene's-eye perspective. Dawkins's much-discussed thesis is that genes are fundamentally "selfish" inasmuch as it is in the interest of a gene to replicate itself. It is precisely this task of genetic replication that is at stake in natural selection, he argues, and not the well-being of a given individual, group, or species. Thus, any act of altruism carried out by an individual animal will likely be a behavior that is ultimately (that is, biologically) selfish inasmuch as it enhances the replication of selfish genes.

So, perhaps, if we follow Dawkins, Levinas is correct after all. Perhaps animals are nothing more than beings whose actions are ultimately grounded in selfish interests—if not at the level of the species or the individual then at the genetic level. Maybe animals and the rest of the individuals that constitute the natural world are simply caught up in a blind and ruthless struggle for existence. And maybe Bobby's gestures toward the prisoners can be explained in the final instance as unconscious behaviors and strategies that are in the service of replicating a certain combination of genes. Perhaps. But there are two consequences that follow from adopting this kind of biological approach to understanding altruism. First, although Dawkins focuses primarily on animal altruism and selfishness, the theory of the selfish gene captures both animals and humans within its sweep. Like Darwin before him, Dawkins is a staunch advocate of biological continuism and refuses to make any exceptions for human beings within his explanatory framework.[6] Thus, if adopted, the selfish-gene theory would render both human and animal altruism biologically selfish—even (or, perhaps especially) the holiness and being-for-the-Other that Levinas associates with the human. The second consequence, though, is that Dawkins's analysis is not, nor is it intended to be, exhaustive of the phenomenon of altruism. It is simply a *biological* analysis of altruism aimed at explaining the reproductive effects of a given behavior; it has nothing to say about the *psychology* of motives or what is going on at the cognitive level of individuals engaged in altruistic acts.[7] It is thus possible, even on Dawkins's account, that what appears to be altruism in certain animal species *actually is altruism;* perhaps certain animal acts do proceed from the kind of genuine emotional and ethical responsivity that Darwin insists can be found well beyond the human.

Cognitive ethologists take up the question of altruism precisely at this point, where a distinction is drawn between a reductive, gene's-eye-perspective analysis and a more robust, multilayered biological and psychological account of animal behavior. Frans de Waal, a cognitive ethologist who has written extensively on the biological and animal origins of human morality, argues that altruism among animals must be understood in a more encompassing manner. His chief thesis is that altruism should be explained in psychological and biological terms *at several levels* (relations among kin, reciprocity between individuals in social groups, and so forth) and that such explanations do nothing to undercut Darwin's insistence that animal altruism, like human altruism, is genuinely ethical. If anything, de Waal argues, a more complete analysis of animal behavior only *confirms* Darwin's point that there is no sharp break between human beings and animals either in terms of cognition or morality.[8]

Whether the kind of approach that cognitive ethologists such as de Waal advocate will eventually be subsumed by neobehaviorism or a reductionistic version of evolutionary psychology remains to be seen. It is not my intention to enter into these debates here. Rather, my point is this: no matter from which direction we approach the question of animal altruism (reductionist or holistic, biological or psychological), it will be impossible fully to uphold Levinas's version of the idea that animal life as *opposed* to human life is a struggle for existence without ethics. If, following Levinas, we allow for the idea that a genuine displacement of egoism is possible among human beings (if only at the psychological level), then we should be prepared to consider the same possibility with regard to animals.

Levinas's efforts to draw a sharp break between human beings and animals on this issue is not just bad biology—it is also bad philosophy, inasmuch as it uncritically reinforces the metaphysical anthropocentrism of the Western philosophical tradition. To contest such anthropocentrism, it is not necessary to establish a complete homology between human beings and animals around the question of ethical agency, and that has most certainly not been my aim here. At stake rather is an effort to move beyond the reductive vision of animals that we have inherited from the dominant philosophical tradition running from Aristotle and Descartes through Heidegger and Levinas. Such a transformation cannot be achieved in one go or by fiat. It is necessary to make use of the tools at our disposal and to develop them in such a way as to deepen the crisis of metaphysical anthropocentrism and push beyond the limits it has established for thought. In view of this task, the commitment to biological continuism we find in such thinkers as Darwin, Dawkins, and de Waal is an essential path for thought, inasmuch as it both decenters the human and offers the possibility of uncovering traits among animals that were long assumed to be the exclusive province of human beings. The *philosophical* task we are presented with in the face of such discoveries consists in marking and recording these ruptures within philosophical discourse and in extending and deepening them so as to displace the anthropocentric-epistemological thrust that has dominated and continues to dominate the overwhelming majority of philosophical inquiry.

In taking up this task, and in rethinking the way in which the human-animal distinction has been drawn, we are confronted with the fact that Western philosophy—which from its "origins" in Greek thought has grounded itself on a hierarchical version of the human-animal distinction—is constituted irreducibly and essentially as an anthropocentric ethical and political discourse. Not only has the human perspective been taken uncritically as the point of departure for nearly all epistemological inquiry, but the ultimate stakes of engaging with philosophical questions has been subordinated primarily, if not exclusively, to human interests. To mark a rupture in the human-animal distinction, as biology and several other discourses and practices have done, is to announce the fact that philosophy cannot proceed with business as usual. Philosophy can no longer in good conscience ground itself on the assumption that human perspectives and human interests constitute the primary locus for thought. In short, today philosophy finds itself *faced by animals,* a sharp reversal of the classical philosophical gaze. What philosophy is now encountering, and what Levinas's philosophy tries desperately but unsuccessfully to block or dissimulate, is the simple fact that we know neither what animals can do nor what they might become.

It is only by shutting animals "away in a class" and depriving "them of expression"—as Levinas's captors did to him and his fellow prisoners and as he in turn tries to do with animals—that we could have ever thought otherwise. Thus, to do philosophy today means proceeding from and in view of the rupture in the human-animal distinction that has grounded thought thus far. In decentering the human, and by thinking from out of a new humility and generosity toward what we call "the nonhuman," a genuinely nonanthropocentric thought might be developed.

To approach nonhuman animals in this manner, however, is already to grant the notion that animals might have the capacity to initiate something like an ethical encounter, an encounter in which an animal could strike a human being as radically Other and challenge the categories under which human thought and practice might place a given animal. Such an encounter would mean that the animal could have a "face" in the Levinasian sense, which is to say, an expressivity and vulnerability that calls my thought and egoism into question and that demands an alternative mode of relation. This possibility returns us to the second question posed at the outset of this section, the question concerning whether nonhuman animals are the kinds of beings that elicit an ethical response in human beings. Despite the growing body of work on animal ethics that take such experiences for granted, the dominant thrust of Levinas's writings seems to deny that an ethical interruption coming from an animal is possible. Again, the conclusion that Levinas draws here is not surprising given the priority he places on interhuman ethics. But his anthropocentrism is equivocal along these lines as well. For although Levinas argues explicitly that the Other can only be another human being, his account of ethical experience does not permit him to establish this boundary with any rigor. Furthermore, when directly challenged by interviewers on the possibility of an ethical encounter with an animal, even Levinas is unable to deny that an animal might have a face. Let me unpack these two points in more detail.

Levinas's most detailed discussion of the idea that the Other can only be another human being is found in *Totality and Infinity*, in the section devoted to "Discourse."[9] Here he is concerned to make the point that the ethical relation presupposes an absolute (and not just a relative) difference between the Same and the Other. Levinas argues that in order for an absolute difference to exist between me and the Other, there must be some aspect of both me and the Other that resists being integrated within a single purview. On my side, the side of the Same, it is my particular mode of enjoyment that cannot be captured by the perspective of a third-party observer. The entire egoistic process whereby I firm myself up and become a subject is uniquely mine and constitutes my secret interiority, my ipseity. Although I am constantly in relation with others (both human and nonhuman) and continuously immersed in an elemental milieu throughout this developmental process, these "others" upon which I am dependent only *influence* and *condition* me; they do not, according to Levinas, fundamentally *interrupt* me or my egoistic pursuits. And with the eventual establishment of a dwelling place of my own, I am able to overcome almost all of the insecurities that plague my egoistic pursuits. My home gives me the time and space to re-collect myself, protects me from the elements, and allows for the objects of enjoyment fully to become my possessions.

My encounter with the face of the Other interrupts all of this—and in a fundamental manner. Through this encounter, my "animal complacency" (*TI*, 149) is put in check; my projects are derailed; my house becomes a hostel; and my possessions are transformed into gifts. The question that arises at this point is: Who is capable of interrupting my egoism in this manner? Who could provide this kind of shock? Who is this Other? For the Other to be a genuine and absolute Other— something that Levinas maintains is essential to the ethicality of the encounter—the Other cannot belong to *any* genus whatsoever, not even one as broad as "humanity." So it will not do to say simply that the Other is another human being. Levinas, of course, recognizes this point, and this is why his humanism is not based on a biological or anthropological concept of humanity. Of course, the Other is in fact, for Levinas, what is ordinarily called a "human" being, but human being here should be understood as denoting those entities who are incapable of being fully reduced to the Same's projects and objective intentionality. The human, then, is an *ethical* concept rather than a species concept; consequently, the concept of the human could—at least in principle—be extended well beyond human beings to include other kinds of beings who call my egoism into question.

Were Levinas to stick strictly with the idea that the human is simply a name that represents those beings who disrupt my egoism, then the human would function in a manner analogous to the concept of the "the feminine" in *Totality and Infinity,* where the feminine stands as an empty placeholder for the intimacy and welcoming that occurs with my be-loved in the home, a place that could presumably be occupied by either gender. Of course, as several feminist readers of Levinas have pointed out, this concept of the feminine is problematic, even when understood charitably, for gendered concepts almost never function neutrally in the way Levinas might wish. Likewise, we could say that "the human," even if understood charitably as the placeholder for *any* being that challenges my egoism, is nevertheless a problematic concept inasmuch as the con-cept of the human carries significant metaphysical and ethical baggage. As we have seen, though, Levinas does *not* limit himself to the modest claim that the human is an empty placeholder. He maintains, and with considerable resoluteness, that the Other is and can only be an actual *human* Other.

In the section of *Totality and Infinity* I have been examining, Levinas underscores this point by drawing a distinction between human beings and nonhuman beings (referred to in this section as "things") and ar-guing for the exclusive priority of the former in the ethical sphere. His thesis here is that "the absolutely foreign alone can instruct me. And the absolutely foreign can only be man" (*TI*, 73). In other words, it is only the absolute Other who is able to pierce through my egoistic buffer and call my egoism into question. But why is "man alone" capable of bringing about this interruption? According to Levinas, the human Other is the only Other who cannot be reduced, in the final analysis, to my projects. In encountering a vulnerable human Other, my ambitions are placed in check. I meet with a resistance that is greater than any strength I might muster in order to counter its force. Were I so inclined, I could enslave, abuse, or even slaughter this vulnerable human Other, but, paradoxically, it is the very vulnerability of the Other that *dis*inclines me to do so and gives me pause. The Other calls to me as if "from on high," from a loca-tion that reverses my mastery over the Other into a freely chosen ethical servitude. In the encounter with the Other, my objective intentionality and egoistic ipseity are unlinked, or rather relinked along ethical lines and called toward justice and hospitality.

By contrast, Levinas insists that *non*human entities, no matter how much resistance they might offer to my egoism, are unable to call me into question in any significant way. Whatever resistance they might offer can ultimately be overcome, either through my strength or through technological assistance. Of course, nature and artifacts do not always enter my sphere of concern ready-made for the projects and tasks that I have set for myself, but they can usually be bent and forced in that direction when necessary. And if, in the end, they fail to fit within my sphere of concern, they can always be left or tossed aside. What is important to understand here is that, on Levinas's analysis, *the resistance of nonhuman things does not make any ethical impact on me.* When nonhuman things resist me, they do not do so because they are "free" or because they are able by themselves to resist my categorization—for nonhuman entities have no *presence* outside of a human context. In other words, things have no presence *kath auto;* they take on sense only in reference to a specific human task or context. Consequently, within Levinas's phenomenological approach, nonhuman beings can come to presence in many forms: as instruments, furnishings, objects of enjoyment or beauty, gifts to be offered to the human Other in need, even as the anonymous matter of the *il y a.* But they can never pierce me ethically or interrupt my functioning in such a way as to challenge my persistence in being.

Whether this analysis of the nonethicality of things is adequate can certainly be questioned.[10] Levinas himself seems to glimpse the possibility of things having a quasi-ethical presence on more than one instance, most famously at the end of "Is Ontology Fundamental?" where he asks "Can things take on a face?"[11] But this possibility is nowhere taken seriously in his mature work,[12] and it never overrides the priority he grants to the human face. So, if things by and large lack a face according to Levinas, what can be said of animal faces? Many of the beings we would call "animal" do not seem to fit neatly within the category of things as Levinas describes them (almost all of Levinas's examples of things are what we are commonly called "inanimate objects": the cigarette lighter, eyeglasses, and so on); yet he most assuredly would not want to assimilate animals to human beings at the ethical level. So where to place animals within the phenomenology of ethical life that Levinas provides?

Levinas is pushed to address this issue explicitly in the interview I mentioned above, "The Paradox of Morality." Levinas's interviewers here ask him point blank whether the Other might be an other animal, whether the human face is distinct from the animal face, and whether human beings have obligations to nonhuman animals. Levinas's responses to these questions display a certain confusion on his part, but they are extremely instructive in helping to tease out his position on the issue of animal ethics. On the whole, his responses are quite generous, especially given his near complete avoidance of the topic in his major works. Levinas grants initially that "one cannot entirely refuse the face of an animal," but he maintains that the animal face is secondary to and derivative of our encounter with the human face: "The priority here is not found in the animal, but in the human face. We understand the animal, the face of an animal, in accordance with Dasein."[13] What is more interesting than these ungrounded claims about the priority of the human face, however, is Levinas's equivocation on the *extent* of animal ethics. Are we to understand the idea that "one cannot entirely refuse the face of an animal" as implying that *all* animals have a face, or is it only certain animals that present themselves with ethical force? Levinas's main example in his discussion of the animal face is a dog (we don't know if he has Bobby specifically in mind), in which he finds both a vital force and a vulnerability evoking pity. It is this latter aspect that leads him to say explicitly that the dog "has a face." But immediately following this comment, Levinas becomes agnostic about the matter of how far this thinking extends: "I cannot say at what moment you have the right to be called 'face'. I don't know if a snake has a face. I can't answer that question."[14] To complicate matters even further, Levinas follows this agnostic position with a positive and confident extension of ethical consideration to *all life forms*: "It is clear that, without considering animals as human beings, the ethical extends to all living beings."[15]

So what are we to make of this contradiction between an agnosticism concerning the extent of animal ethics and the confident extension of the ethical to all living beings? It is no doubt tempting for many who are, like I am, inclined toward a robust animal and environmental ethics to dismiss Levinas's agnosticism and to embrace his nod toward biocentrism. Adopting the latter approach would allow for the development of a phenomenological ethics of nature based on the interruptive force of diverse kinds of nonhuman life.[16] But I want to suggest that this move, which is becoming increasingly de rigueur in Continental environmental philosophy, leads to a dead end and should be avoided for several reasons. Furthermore, I believe that Levinas's agnosticism provides a more promising avenue for ethical thought as it seeks to move beyond the limits imposed by an anthropocentric approach. Let me defend these two claims in more detail.

On Universal Consideration;
Or, Ethics Without A Priori Content

Ethics, if we follow the analysis of Levinas undertaken thus far, can be generally defined as an interruption of my egoism coming from the face of Other that transforms my being in the direction of generosity. In other words, ethics combines responsivity to the face with an enacted responsibility. Levinas's most common examples of ethics are typically focused on the way in which the Other's destitution and vulnerability call my spontaneity into question and lead me to give up my possessions (for example, the bread "painfully torn" from my mouth) in order to ameliorate the Other's suffering. In his later writings, Levinas increasingly describes ethics in terms of my being called to being-for-the-Other in the face of the Other's death. But in both cases, the formal structure of ethics remains the same: it involves a disruption of my perseverance in being that deeply affects and transforms my entire existence such that the Other becomes my priority. And yet there is no reason to think that ethics should be *restricted* to such encounters. Levinas has every right, of course, to stress the ethical force of the encounter with the Other's destitution or of being faced by the Other's finitude. Not only are these instances quintessentially ethical, but they speak to the particular historicopolitical events that inform his work. There is no reason to believe, however, that ethics as such is *exhausted* by such encounters. There are any number of ways in which my egoism might be interrupted, any number of kinds of entities that might disrupt me, and any number of ways I might be transformed by such encounters—several of which could just as suitably be called "ethical" as the ones Levinas highlights. Indeed, Levinas's equivocations on the possibility of things and animals having a face points in this very direction. That he focuses on what he takes to be the specificity and priority of the human face is, if not wholly defensible in philosophical terms, certainly understandable. But there is no need to restrict our attention in the same manner.

What would ethics look like, then, if we took seriously Levinas's definition but lifted the idiosyncratic restrictions he places on the ethical encounter? Simply put, ethics would become rigorously and generously *agnostic*. But what exactly does this mean? If we follow the distinctions I made above among the ways in which my egoism might be interrupted, the kinds of entities who might call me into question, and the manner in which such interruptions might transform me, it is clear that the central issue concerning agnosticism revolves around the second point: the kinds of entities who might call me into question. I assume that most readers of Levinas who are somewhat sympathetic to his project would be generous in allowing for alternative modes of interruption (the first point) and transformation (the third point) as belonging to a given ethical encounter. An ethical interruption could proceed from an encounter with the Other's kindness or vitality as much as from his or her destitution or finitude. There does not seem to be any way of enumerating a priori the various kinds of encounters that might derail my egoism and push me toward responsibility, and one would be hard pressed to argue that ethics could *only* occur through the examples Levinas typically employs. Likewise, the transformations of my specific mode of being that follow from an ethical encounter will not always take the standard Levinasian form of a responsibility that involves giving "with both hands." Sometimes an ethical response might involve simply leaving the Other alone, or perhaps joining with the Other in celebration or protest, to name just a few possible responses. The points I am making here are, I hope, obvious ones to readers familiar with the logic of Levinas's ethical philosophy.

What is more difficult to come to grips with is *who* the Other is who might call me into question. Here, too, I think a rigorous and generous agnosticism is called for, but it is around this question that the greatest difficulty arises. For how, precisely, are we to think about alterity along these lines? Surely the Other cannot be *infinite* in this sense, too, without *any* definable limits a priori, and capable of taking *any* form? As we have seen, Levinas maintains for the most part that the human answers to the question of the "Who?" of the Other. But his equivocations on this question have led us to look beyond the human and toward other Others. So where does this search end? In contemporary moral philosophy, this question has been discussed at length under the rubric of determining the criterion of "moral considerability," which is to say, the criterion that establishes the necessary and sufficient conditions that must be met for an entity to be considered worthy of practical respect.[17] In recent years, and in view of the challenges posed by feminists and animal and environmental ethicists to classical conceptions of moral considerability, moral philosophers have sought to determine this criterion with increased rigor. And there has been no shortage of answers offered. Philosophers have proposed drawing the line at every imaginable level, including those of beings with moral agency, sentient human beings and animals, humans and animals who are subjects-of-a-life, all living organisms, beings capable of reciprocal caring relationships, ecosystems, and even mere existence. Such monistic theories of moral considerability have even been joined recently by multicriterial accounts that seek to gather together the strongest elements of these various criteria into a pluralistic framework.[18] Given the line of thought I am pursuing here, that of a rigorous and generous agnosticism concerning the "who" of the Other, we could say charitably that all of the above efforts at determining moral considerability are useful for highlighting how particular entities (individualistic criteria) or networks of interaction (holistic criteria) might have an ethical claim on us; likewise, these criteria give an abundance of reasons why we should attend to the various kinds of beings and relationships that are under discussion. At the same time, however, there is something fundamentally wrong with this entire approach to moral consideration, *for it proceeds as if the question of moral consideration is one that permits of a final answer.* If ethics arises from an encounter with an Other who is fundamentally irreducible to and unanticipatable by my egoistic and cognitive machinations, then how could this question ever be answered once and for all? By what right can we delimit who the Other is in advance of such encounters? Should we not, then, take Levinas literally when he says "I cannot say at what moment you have the right to be called 'face'"?

If this is indeed the case, that is, if it is the case that we do not know where the face begins and ends, where moral considerability begins and ends, then we are obliged to proceed from the possibility that *anything* might take on a face. And we are further obliged to hold this possibility permanently open. At this point, most reasonable readers will likely see the argument I have been making as having absurd consequences. While it might not be unreasonable to consider the possibility that "higher" animals who are "like" us, animals who have sophisticated cognitive and emotive functions, could have a moral claim on us, are we also to believe that "lower" animals, insects, dirt, hair, fingernails, ecosystems, and so on could also have a claim on us? Any argument that leads to this possibility is surely a reductio ad absurdum. In response to such a charge, I would suggest affirming and embracing what the critic sees as an absurdity. All attempts to shift or enlarge the scope of moral consideration are initially met with the same reactionary rejoinder of absurdity from those who uphold common sense. But any thought worthy of the name, especially any thought of *ethics,* takes its point of departure in setting up a critical relation to common sense and the established *doxa* and, as such, *demands* that we ponder absurd, unheard-of thoughts. Moreover, is not ethics itself, in a certain sense, an absurd pursuit, governed by a "logic" that defies logic? Is it reason that opens an ethical encounter or that convinces me to set aside my egoism? Levinas tells us that the opening to ethics is beyond reason and that it is not a "particularly recommendable" variety of consciousness precisely because it overrides any reasonable conception of responsibility. What is more, the reductio cuts both ways here. We could ask in turn: Is it at all reasonable to conclude that there is a rational or objective way to determine the limits of moral consideration? And does not a historical survey of the failures that have attended every such attempt to draw *the* line (or lines) of moral considerability provide enough evidence to persuade even common sense that this approach is inherently pernicious, both morally and politically?

Thomas Birch makes a similar set of points about the problematic aspects of the moral-considerability debate in his essay "Moral Considerability and Universal Consideration."[19] He notes that from a "historical perspective, we see that whenever we have closed off the question [of moral considerability] with the institution of some practical criterion, we have later found ourselves in error, and have had to open the question up again to reform our practices in a further attempt to make them ethical" (MC, 321). The lesson that Birch draws from this historical perspective parallels the point I have been making with and against Levinas thus far: the question of who the Other is, that is, of who might make a claim on me and thus be morally considerable, cannot be determined with any finality. Unless we proceed from this kind of generous agnosticism, not only are we bound to make mistakes (who would be bold enough to claim that rationality or phenomenology will overcome our finitude and specific historical location in making such judgments?), but we also set up the conditions of possibility for the worst kinds of abuses toward those beings who are left outside the scope of moral concern. As Birch explains, the main problem with much of moral theory and practice is that it is premised on the belief that there *should* be an inside and outside with regard to moral considerability. Moral theory and practice have presupposed (1) that when it comes to moral considerability, there *are*, and *ought* to be, insiders and outsiders, citizens and non-citizens (for examples, slaves, barbarians, and women), "members of the club" of *consideranda* versus the rest; (2) that we *can* and *ought* to identify the mark, or marks, of membership; (3) that we *can* identify them in a rational and non-arbitrary fashion; and (4) that we *ought* to institute practices that enforce the marks of membership and the integrity of the club, as well, of course, as maximizing the good of its members.

(MC 315)

That these presuppositions betray a rather unethical, even imperialistic starting point, coupled with the fact they have served as the ground for some of the worst atrocities human beings have committed, should be enough to make us rethink this approach to ethics from the ground up. Futhermore, it is not at all clear that ethical *experience* permits such neat and tidy divisions of who does and does not count, of where my concern should begin and end, and of who has a face and who does not. And is this not the chief lesson of Levinas's thought? If we are to learn anything from Levinas, it is that ethical experience occurs precisely where phenomenology is interrupted and that ethical experience is traumatic and not easily captured by thought. Given its diachronic structure, ethical experience can at best be only partially reconstructed in thetic form. This would, it seems, require us always to proceed *as if* we might have missed or misinterpreted the Other's trace.

Rather than trying to determine the definitive criterion or criteria of moral considerability, we might, following Birch and the reading of Levinas I have been pursuing, begin from a notion of "universal consideration" that takes seriously our fallibility in determining where the face begins and ends. Universal consideration would entail being ethically attentive and open to the possibility that anything might take on a face; it would also entail taking up a skeptical and critical relation to the determinations of moral consideration that form the contours of our present-day moral thinking. Universal consideration is, as Birch suggests, a matter of "giving others of all sorts a chance to reveal their value, and of giving ourselves a chance to see it, rather than approaching them in hostility as if they have nothing but negative value until they have proved otherwise" (MC 328).

It is important to stress that this notion of universal consideration does not make the positive claim that all things or all life forms *do* count as the ethical Other; nor does it supply any positive claim concerning *how* various beings or relational structures might count. On both points, an ethics of universal consideration requires us to keep the question wide open. By contrast, most of the attempts made thus far to use Levinas's thought to explore animal and environmental ethics have abandoned this kind of agnosticism regarding where the face begins and ends. They have sought to establish a homology between the suffering and distress of animals or the environment, on the one hand, and human suffering, on the other hand, and then argued for a kind of ethical extensionism from the human to the nonhuman based on parity of reasoning. While I certainly have sympathy for such approaches up to a point, it is important to examine these arguments carefully, inasmuch as they have a tendency to close the door on the question of where the face begins and ends and the various ways in which an ethical interruption might take place.

If such caution is in fact required, then the question that arises is: Why have I been discussing *animal* ethics at all? Is this term not just as problematic as "the human" or "life"? And why limit the discussion just to animals? Why not cast the net wider? Or, if we take the notion of universal consideration seriously, why *name* the Other at all? The brief answer, and one that I will try to explain and defend in what follows, is that it is necessary to take such risks. Contemporary ethical discourse and practice do not take place in a vacuum, but emerge from out of a series of background practices and beliefs that have placed the interests of animals outside the scope of moral and political considerability. In order to challenge the established order of things along this line, it is necessary to take up the terms of the discourse as they currently stand and transform them. There are, then, several different reasons for focusing on the animal question in particular:

1. *The strategic disruption of metaphysical anthropocentrism:* One of the chief limitations for thought at present is "metaphysical anthropocentrism," or the tendency to determine nonhuman life in an oppositional and hierarchical manner with respect to the human. Nowhere is this problem more evident than in our thinking on the human-animal distinction. This site, perhaps more than any other (for example, human-machine, human-divine, human-environment, and so on), is the source of mas-

argument for why this question needs to be treated first...

sive anxiety, inasmuch as our increasing knowledge of and familiarity with animals threatens not just to blur but to eliminate this distinction altogether. As anthropocentrism with respect to animals becomes ever less tenable, anthropocentrism of other sorts is also called into question. In this sense, the animal question is one of the primary sites that must be passed through on the way toward another thought of human and nonhuman life, a thought that will perhaps do away with or be unconcerned to think in terms of "the human" and its "others."

2. *The alterity of animals*: Philosophical discourse on animals, including Levinas's, has been overwhelmingly reductionistic and essentialist in its approach. Animals have often been thought of by philosophers as belonging to a single class of beings that lack some essential human trait (language, a concept of death, moral agency, and so on). Not only does this approach gloss over the enormous differences that exist among animals themselves, it also offers a false characterization of the (nonessential) differences between human beings and animals (because there is no single, insuperable dividing line). To focus carefully on the ethical aspects of our interactions with animals forces us to return to this issue with more care than philosophers have traditionally taken. In so doing, we are confronted with the singularity and alterity of animals, with the fact that the beings we call animals do not fit into the categories under which we have placed them. It is because we do not know what animals can do (empirically) or what they might become (ontologically) that animals exceed our conceptualization. And it is precisely in the breakdown of this process of conceptualization that the *ethical* alterity of animals comes to the fore.

3. *Reconfiguring the link between the animal question and environmental issues*: Historically, animal ethicists have set themselves at odds with other forms of ethics that move beyond the human, particularly with environmental ethics. Animal ethicists have, by and large, presented themselves as individualists, whereas the dominant forms of environmental ethics have taken a holistic or relational approach, with each camp pointing out the other's limitations. This difference has led to sharp divisions both in theory and practice. If, however, we address the question of animal ethics from the neo-Levinasian approach developed here, then such divisions get recast in a very different light. Animal ethics becomes but

one way among others of thinking through ethics, with specific attention given to the manner in which various animals might have a claim on us and what consequences follow from responding to such claims. That other kinds of beings, systems, or relational structures might have a claim on us is not ruled out but rather is allowed in principle under an ethics of universal consideration. Thus, rather than being in opposition to each other, animal ethics and environmental ethics would be seen as two distinct but complementary forms of ethical inquiry and practice that seek to challenge the limits of anthropocentrism.

4. *The situation of animals themselves:* Perhaps it goes without saying, but it should nevertheless be stressed that the animal question is particularly pressing given the present conditions under which many animals exist. Never before in human history have so many animals been subjected to horrific slaughter, unconscionable abuse, and unthinkable living conditions. The present conditions under which many animals live has a unique history that requires both material and ontological analysis, and it is a history that needs to be attended to in its *specificity* so that we might learn better how to transform it for the present and the future. Certainly, this does not mean that the history of the subjection of animals should not be thought alongside the history of other interrelated forms of oppression, examples of which we find in the writings of ecofeminists and other progressive animal rights theorists. The work offered here should be seen as proceeding in the same spirit and in deep solidarity with these approaches. But I also wish to underscore that the animal question cannot be fully reduced to or made identical with other human struggles against oppression. The logics of domination overlap at points, but they also diverge—and both the convergences and divergences are equally important for thought and practice. Likewise, we need to pay specific attention to the unique ways in which animals themselves resist subjection and domination, even if their efforts are not wholly successful. The elephant who escapes from its imprisonment at a circus; the pig who flees the slaughterhouse and runs free in the streets until shot by police; the whales who protect each other from harpoons; the lion who mauls its human handler; the chimpanzee who attacks an experimental scientist; the feral cat who refuses to be handled; Bobby the dog surviving against all odds in "some wild patch in the region of the camp"—these and other such figures of animal resistance should remain at the core of animal

ethics as much as the suffering animals whose terrible fate we indirectly catch sight of at meal time or in underground videos of slaughterhouses.

So, the approach to animal ethics outlined here differs from the standard Levinasian approaches mentioned above in not seeing itself as developing *the* criterion or criteria by which something takes on a face. Rather, animal ethics is seen here as a *risk,* a "fine risk" of the sort Levinas speaks of in *Otherwise Than Being: Or Beyond Essence.* It is a risk to focus on animals, even when this focus is open-ended and generously agnostic. It is a risk to constrain our thinking to focus on the specific history of animal subjection and resistance, even when such histories are viewed in conjunction with other histories of struggle and oppression. There are no guarantees that we have gotten things right here or that this particular approach will in fact have the kind of transformative effect we might desire. But such risks are what constitute the act of doing philosophy. They are fine risks, risks taken in the name of "the Other animal" and without any pretension to fully representing or understanding those singular beings we call animals.

CHAPTER THREE

Jamming the Anthropological Machine

Agamben

INTRODUCTION

Giorgio Agamben arrived at his recent work on the question of the animal through a rather circuitous route. Similar to Martin Heidegger and Emmanuel Levinas, much of Agamben's early focus was on the question of thinking through the remains of human propriety in the wake of the decentering of human subjectivity. In his writings from the 1970s, 1980s, and 1990s, Agamben elaborates a complicated and provocative account of being human that seeks, again like Heidegger and Levinas, to be genuinely postmetaphysical and posthumanist. However, as this project develops over the decades, it seems to become increasingly clear to Agamben that the aim of trying to specify what constitutes being human is, at bottom, an ontologically bankrupt and politically pernicious project. Indeed, by the time that Agamben takes up the question of the animal explicitly in his 2002 book *L'aperto: L'uomo e l'animale* (*The Open: Man and Animal*), the aim of seeking a postmetaphysical definition of the human is all but abandoned, and reliance on the human-animal distinction that serves as the foundation for Western political and metaphysical thought becomes, on Agamben's reading, the chief obstacle for a postmetaphysical concept of relation and community. My aim in this chapter is to track the itinerary of the formation and eventual abandonment of the human-animal distinction in Agamben's work and to examine the critical and theoretical upshot of this question as it emerges in his most recent texts on the question of the animal.

Agamben's work has a point of departure that is heavily indebted to Heidegger. Not only does he follow Heidegger's view that the Western metaphysical tradition is nihilistic, he also accepts the premise that the ground of this nihilism is to be found in a specific interpretation of human subjectivity that has been dominant in this tradition. And yet, Agamben insists that Heidegger's thought contains within it serious limitations that render impossible his desire to think beyond the confines of the metaphysical tradition. In particular, Agamben suggests that what binds Heidegger's thought irreducibly to the metaphysical tradition he seeks to delimit is an inability to think the ground of, or opening to, human being and language in nonnegative terms. Consequently, in his efforts to challenge the limitations of Heidegger's project and the metaphysical tradition, many of Agamben's early texts are focused on trying to think the ground of the human beyond the negativity characteristic of Heidegger's approach and the metaphysical tradition. Agamben's overarching aim in these works is to "find an experience of speech that no longer presupposes any negative foundation."[1] He finds this nonnegative, or affirmative, ground of being human in the concept of "infancy" (from *infari* and *infans,* the being who does not speak), which in turn opens onto a conception of the human as a fundamentally ethical and political being.

One of the recurring quotations in Agamben's writings derives from book 1, part 2, of Aristotle's *Politics.* In this passage, we encounter one of the earliest efforts in the metaphysical tradition to articulate the relationship between human language and social and political life:

> Now, that man is more of a political animal than bees or any other gregarious animals is evident. Nature, as we often say, makes nothing in vain, and man is the only animal who has the gift of speech. And whereas mere voice is but an indication of pleasure or pain, and is therefore found in other animals (for their nature attains to the perception of pleasure and pain and the intimation of them to one another, and no further), the power of speech is intended to set forth the expedient and inexpedient, and therefore likewise the just and the unjust. And it is a characteristic of man that he alone has any sense of

good and evil, of just and unjust, and the like, and the association of living beings who have this sense makes a family and a state.[2]

Aristotle here posits an inextricable link between human speech and politics and suggests that the ability to make articulate judgments about ethical and social matters is essential to the constitution of a polis. But what interests Agamben in this passage is what remains *unsaid.* In particular, what is it about human beings that makes them capable of speech and different from animals in this regard? Why is the space of transition between animal voice and human speech left unthought by Aristotle?

In his early book *Language and Death,* Agamben presents a series of novel arguments aimed at demonstrating that these questions go largely unanswered throughout the history of the metaphysical tradition. And in those places where the questions are addressed, the ground of human language and social life remains mired in obscurity and negativity. Thus, the link posited by Aristotle between human speech and political life is maintained by metaphysics, but the *ground* of this relation never receives a rigorous formulation. And it is precisely the failure to think through the ground of and relation between human speech and politics that, according to Agamben, ensures the nihilistic consequences of metaphysics.

The difficulty here lies with specifying the precise nature of the "space" of transition between animal voice (understood as instinctual code) and human language (understood as articulate, creative, recursive speech). Agamben argues that the dominant means of doing so in the metaphysical tradition has been to treat the space of transition as ineffable, as a mystical site in which the human encounters a mysterious "Voice." The Voice guarantees the passage from animality to humanity, ensuring that the seeming a-poria between voice and language is transformed into a eu-poria. This Voice, which has the negative characteristics of being no-longer-animal-code and not-yet-articulate-human-speech, appears in varying modes throughout the metaphysical tradition running from medieval thought through modernity and Hegelian philosophy. Whatever variations one might find in this complex history, one thing remains essentially the same for Agamben: the conditions of possibility for the emergence of the human in language are always thought by the metaphysical tradition in nonpositive terms, that is, as ineffable, mystical, negative, and so forth. This remains the case even with Heidegger, who is typically taken to be the postmetaphysical thinker par excellence. Despite the fact that Heidegger seeks to eliminate the idea of *any* link between animality and human essence (and thereby eliminates the problem of explaining the leap from voice to language), he remains trapped within a thematic of the Voice and negativity (primarily in the form of the all-too-mystical and "silent" Voice of conscience) when trying to articulate the uniquely human experience of and opening to language and finitude.

As a consequence, neither Heidegger nor the rest of the metaphysical tradition are able to think human sociality—which, as Aristotle suggests, is tied intimately to the capacity for language—in positive terms. The negative link between language and politics, between the opening to language and the finite opening to alterity (culture, history, and so on), remains the unthought ground upon which metaphysics proceeds. And it is here that Agamben locates the nihilism specific to the tradition. It is a nihilism not in the Nietzschean sense of a declining culture or in the Heideggerian sense of a forgetting of the gift of Being but rather a nihilism stemming from the oblivion and covering over of the political and social "habits" of the human. The nihilism of metaphysics coincides, then, with what Jean-Luc Nancy and Philippe Lacoue-Labarthe call the "retreat of the political," the withdrawal of the thought of what gives rise to politics. Agamben argues that it is only through a "liquidation" of metaphysical mysticism and negativity that thought can begin to find the words for the essential link between speech and politics. In so doing, thought has to learn to dwell in the *infancy* of the human, a task that Agamben takes up in *Infancy and History*.[3]

Agamben approaches the concept of infancy in *Infancy and History* through an examination of modern theories of human subjectivity in which the link between subjectivity and politics posited by Aristotle and classical metaphysics is largely eclipsed in favor of an epistemological and mathematical approach to understanding the specificity and exceptionalism of the human. Thus the possibility of uncovering the traces of sociality at the heart of the human are here even more obscured. In modern thinkers such as Descartes and Kant (and their successors such as Husserl), the site of subjectivity is sought in a quasi-solipsistic, presocial, prelinguistic site uncontaminated by and discontinuous with historical or social forces. This approach leads, in turn, to the consequent difficulty of trying to determine the precise nature of intersubjectivity and how the human subject is inserted in and relates to historical, cultural, and biological forces. Against such modern conceptions of subjectivity and intersubjectivity, Agamben, following his Heideggerian and poststructuralist counterparts, argues that there is no such uncontaminated space of subjectivity. The subject is always already inserted into and shot through with alterity in the forms of social, linguistic, biological, and historicocultural forces.

Agamben develops this argument through recourse to Émile Benveniste's linguistic theory. Benveniste demonstrates that there is no psychological or physical substance to the "I" or subject, which is to say, the "I" has no material referent. The "I" refers instead to the act of discourse in which it is uttered, and it is only and in and through the utterance of "I" that the "I" has any reality at all. What Benveniste's theory amounts to, in brief, is the notion that the subject who says "I" emerges only *in language* and has no existence or reality outside of language. Thus, the quintessential aim of modern epistemology—the aim of locating the ground of the subject and of epistemology outside the play of language, culture, and history—is, from Benveniste's perspective a priori impossible. If language is absent, there can be no self, and where there *is* a self, there is always already language.[4]

For those theorists who wish to salvage something of agency and subjectivity from this apparent linguistic reductionism and idealism, there is a desire to uncover something of the subject that exceeds language. For if the "I" is simply coextensive with language, then there is no break between the human subject and its linguistic milieu, and thus no human history, culture, or alterity. Stated otherwise, were the human "I" and language fully identical, the human would be in language like "water in water." Georges Bataille uses this phrase to describe the animal's relation to the world, suggesting that animality as such is characterized by its complete immanence in its instinctual and natural surroundings.[5] As we have seen, Heidegger makes a similar point in arguing that the animal is intimately bound with its environment. Are human beings tied to language in a similarly intimate way, such that it would be impossible to mark a sharp break between human beings and animals? The putative break with animal instinct comes, according to much of the Western philosophical tradition, with the acquisition of language. It is because animals lack language that they are unable to break with their environmental and instinctual milieu, or, for Heidegger, the lack of language is indicative of the animal's constitutional lack of finite transcendence. But these standard answers only lead to a dead end because if language is tied intimately to the constitution of the human subject, then there is the risk that the subject is either determined by language (in the sense that language is received from outside the subject and thus structures and determines its "agency" from without) or completely identical with language (in the sense that language is innate, thereby rendering human language identical with animal codes). Either understanding of the relation between language and the human renders the prospect of distinguishing human beings from animals rather difficult.

Although Agamben follows his predecessors in assuming that there *is* a break between the human and the animal with respect to language, he does not assume that animals are without language altogether. Rather, the break between human beings and animals is found within language itself. The human is situated at a site within language where language itself is split, and the "fate" of the human, according to Agamben, is to traverse and move constantly back and forth between this split. The split in language that Agamben has in mind here is the same one we saw in examining *Language and Death*: the split between animal code and articulate human speech, or to use Benveniste's terms, the split between the semiotic and the semantic. Although animal codes have often been thought not to be strictly linguistic, Agamben (following Benveniste and contemporary semiotic theory) insists that animal communication is fully linguistic. From this perspective, the difference between human beings and animals has nothing to do with animals' lacking language. Animals, like human beings, are linguistic beings through and through. The difference between animals and human beings with respect to language is that animals are identical with, and fully immersed in, the language they speak. Animals are in language in the same way that they are in their surrounding environment: like "water in water." In Agamben's words,

> It is not language in general that marks out the human from other living beings—according to the Western metaphysical tradition that sees man as *zoon logon echon* (an animal endowed with speech)—but the split between language and speech, between semiotic and semantic (in Benveniste's sense), between sign system and discourse. Animals are not in fact denied language; on the contrary, they are always and

totally language. . . . Animals do not enter language, they are already inside it.[6]

Consequently, to suggest that human nature is distinguished by its "having language" fails to articulate what is uniquely human. According to Agamben's line of argument, what is unique to human beings is that they are actually *deprived* of language (in the form of articulate speech) and are forced to receive it from outside of themselves. Infancy is the name given to this situation of human beings existing fundamentally in language but without discourse. There is no point at which the human being is in discourse like the animal is in language. And it is this state of being fundamentally deprived of language, this state of infancy, that opens human beings to alterity in the forms of culture, history, and politics.

As I stated at the beginning of this chapter, the overarching thrust of Agamben's early writings is to find a way to think the relational structures of deprivation and infancy in nonnegative, nonnihilistic terms, for he believes that contemporary nihilism stems from the tendency of Western metaphysics to think the ground of human being in negative and mystical terms. As persuasive as this thesis is in many respects, it is necessary to examine the assumptions upon which it is based before accepting it uncritically. First, Agamben follows Heidegger in assuming that historicity (that is, the opening to history) is uniquely human and that, as such, history and everything that follows from it (culture, politics, and so on) is found only among human beings. That this assumption can be contested on empirical grounds is even more obvious today than it was during the time in which Agamben was writing *Infancy and History* (the late 1970s). Indeed, Agamben himself seems to be aware that his remarks on human infancy are complicated by empirical evidence available at the time that suggests a parallel infancy among animals; for it is not at all the case that all animal species are "always and totally" in language. In his remarks on ethologist William Thorpe, Agamben calls attention to the fact that in certain bird species, the acquisition of their "code" is actually partially learned and is not wholly innate, and this is true of the languages of other animal species as well. Furthermore, if we look for signs of "historicity" among nonhuman beings in sites other than language (and that we restrict ourselves to language understood in a literal and reductive manner in examining the issue of historicity is another problematic aspect of the Western logocentric tradition), it is clear that the characteristics and behaviors accompanying historicity (culture, politics) are to be found among a wide range of animal species.[7] The second assumption, which follows from Agamben's first, is that political thought can and should be restricted to human beings. For not only is there no politics among nonhuman animals according to Agamben (a point that follows logically from the argument he makes in *Infancy and History* and one that is explicitly made in multiple texts), but it is unclear what, if any role animals play in human political life. Agamben's early work is structured throughout in such a way as to place human beings at the center of politics and to leave all other beings in abeyance. As I shall argue below, the writings of his middle period continue this trend. But his most recent writings, which will be the focus of the last portion of the chapter, might be to taken to suggest, if one follows the reading of them that I shall propose, that the above assumptions about animal historicity and politics and the more basic thesis of human-animal dualism and discontinuity that underlies them must be abandoned.

Let us return, then, to the development of the human-animal distinction and the question of the animal in Agamben's texts. During the late 1980s and early to mid-1990s, Agamben turns from the issue of articulating the ethicopolitical preconditions of discursive speech to sketching in the contours of an actual politics and concept of community befitting these preconditions. Yet even as he seeks to develop a radically nonessentialist conception of community based on "whatever singularities" and beings devoid of any propriety,[8] Agamben continues in the insistence characteristic of his earlier writings that the site of politics marks a sharp break of human beings from animality. In his 1995 essay "The Face," Agamben uses the motif of *exposition* to name the site of corelation prior to language between persons, a site he argues that is open only to human beings:

> Exposition is the location of politics. If there is no animal politics, that is perhaps because animals are always already in the open and do not try to take possession of their own exposition; they simply live in it without caring about it. That is why they are not interested in mirrors, in the image as image. Human beings, on the other hand, separate images from things and give them a name precisely because they want to recognize themselves, that is, they want to take possession of

their very own appearance. Human beings thus transform the open into a world, that is, into the battlefield of a political struggle without quarter. This struggle, whose object is truth, goes by the name of History.[9]

This passage contains all of the dogmatic elements we have seen in Heidegger's and Levinas's discourse on animals: a simple human-animal distinction; lack of attention to existing empirical knowledge about animals (here the inattention concerns the empirically false claim that animals as such "are not interested in mirrors");[10] and the invariant concern to determine the supposedly unique human relation to the word and history—as if what constitutes the ground of a supposedly unique mode of human existence is the sole (or even primary) thing at stake for philosophical thought.

Variations on these anthropocentric themes abound in Agamben's writings from this period, whether the concept being developed is potentiality, the irreparable, or political refugees. And if one turns to Agamben's texts from this period in the hopes of deepening the anti-humanist critique of *human* subjectivity, the writings are invaluable for undercutting any kind of simplistic neohumanism. But, much like Heidegger and Levinas, Agamben seems unable to connect his critique of humanism with the problem of *anthropocentrism*. His writings exhibit a remarkable critical vigilance toward any effort to develop a dogmatic neohumanism but do not manifest the same vigilance toward anthropocentric determinations of animal life.

Since the mid-1990s, Agamben's work has begun to shift increasingly toward the task of thinking through the links tying sovereignty, law, and the State to the isolation of what he calls *bare life* within human beings. In the development of this project, the question of the animal has begun increasingly to impose itself on Agamben's thought from within. Thus, in *Homo Sacer* we find the logic of the sovereign ban illustrated with the literary motif of the werewolf, a being that is neither human nor animal but rather situated at the margins of the human and the animal and thus marking the constitutive outside of sovereign protection;[11] and in a sequel to *Homo Sacer, Remnants of Auschwitz,* we are confronted with the image of the "Muselmann" (the singular human being at stake in Agamben's post-Auschwitz ethics) who wanders through the Nazi concentration camps like a "stray dog," simultaneously captured inside and outside the force of law.[12] Although these texts fall far short of providing a full analysis of the place of animals within modern biopolitics or the functioning of the human-animal distinction within the logic of sovereignty, the *necessity* for developing such an account seems to be glimpsed here by Agamben.

THE RUPTURE OF ANTHROPOCENTRISM

One of Agamben's more recent works, *The Open: Man and Animal*—which will serve as the primary focus for the remainder of this chapter—partially remedies these deficiencies by exploring the question of the animal at more length.[13] In fact, in this text the issue of the human-animal distinction is granted a preeminent status among the problems facing contemporary political thought. Early in this text, Agamben writes,

> What is man, if he is always the place—and, at the same time, the result—of ceaseless divisions and caesurae? It is more urgent to work on these divisions, to ask in what way—within man—has man been separated from non-man, and the animal from the human, than it is to take positions on the great issues, on so-called human rights and values. (O, 16)

Such remarks are indicative of the steadfast commitment to antihumanism characteristic of the texts from Agamben I have discussed thus far. For him there is little point in pursuing a politics and ethics based on human rights when the full impact of the critique of humanism has not been measured and allowed to transform our ideas of community and being-with others. Inasmuch as humanism is founded on a separation of the *humanitas* and *animalitas* within the human, no genuinely posthumanist politics can emerge without grappling with the logic and consequences of this division. More is at issue here, however, than contesting humanism.

I will examine this last point momentarily, but before doing so, it is important to note that addressing this question alone—namely, the question of how the human-animal distinction functions in determining what it means to be human—will not suffice to call anthropocentrism into question. This is especially true where, as is the case in much of Agamben's writings, one limits the analysis to the manner in which this distinction is played out "within man." If this were all Agamben sought to do in *The Open,* there would be little to distinguish this book from the previous volumes in the *Homo Sacer* series, which analyze the separation of *zoē* and *bíos* within human life only to leave the question of animal life and politics suspended. It seems, then, that if one is to address the philosophical and political question of the animal in any meaningful way, it will be necessary at the very least to work through both the ontology of animal life *on its own terms* and the ethicopolitical relations that obtain between those beings called "human" and "animal."

Although Agamben, like his predecessors in the Continental tradition, has been slow to address the question of the animal from this broader perspective, there are at least two reasons why it must inevitably be engaged in this enlarged form if we are to develop a genuinely posthumanist approach to politics. As is clear from the arguments made in the first two chapters, the posthumanist critique of humanism is to be understood not as a misanthropic or dismissive rejection of the accomplishments of Enlightenment modernism but as a critical investigation of human *subjectivity,* of the material (for example, economic, historical, linguistic, and social) forces at work in the formation of human subjects. Specific to the post-Nietzschean and post-Heideggerian critique of humanism (a lineage to which Agamben clearly belongs) is a probing of the conditions of possibility that render subjects open to material forces as such. But what does it mean to say that one comes to be a subject only in and through language or history? And how must a subject be structured so that it can be affected and transformed by material forces outside of itself? In offering answers to such questions, it quickly becomes clear that the presubjective conditions that give rise to human subjectivity (whether figured as ek-stasis [Heidegger], exposure [Nancy], ex-appropriation [Derrida], or exposition [Agamben]) cannot easily be restricted to human beings. And this is the first reason why antihumanism ultimately opens onto the larger issue of nonhuman animals—for the subjective being of many nonhuman animals, too, is constituted by differential structures of exposure that render standard accounts of the human-animal distinction suspect. At this level of presubjective and prepersonal singularities, there are no clear-cut criteria for distinguishing animal modes of exposure from human modes; what we encounter, rather, are complex networks of relations, affects, and becomings into which both human beings and animals are thrown. As such, posthumanism is confronted with the necessity of returning to first philosophy with the task of creating a nonanthropocentric ontology of life-death, a topic upon which I briefly touched in the discussion of Deleuze and Guattari in chapter 1.

The second chief reason that posthumanists like Agamben must account for the place of animals within their project arises at the ethico-political level. While it is clear that most posthumanist philosophers do not accept in toto standard philosophical theories of value, there can be little doubt that the critique of humanism is motivated by a kind of ethical and political imperative. The assumption by many posthumanists is that nihilism and the major political catastrophes of our age are linked in a profound way with the very humanism typically offered by neohumanists as a solution to these issues. For posthumanists, then, overcoming these problems would require something other than a humanist politics based on a naïve account of human subjectivity. The shared intuition and hope of most posthumanist philosophers seems to be that a less destructive and more sustainable form of politics can be developed beginning from a kind of relational ontology. Here we might take Levinas's project as an example of this approach. Although Levinas is usually approached as a purely ethical thinker, it is also possible and even necessary to read his work in *political* terms, that is, as responding to a political problem. The great danger for Levinas arises when politics becomes unmoored from its ethical grounding and forgets its justification and calling as a response to the face of the Other. By recalling politics to its ethical foundations—which Levinas locates in a presubjective exposure to the Other human—he hopes to reinvigorate and radicalize existing forms of politics (such as liberal democracy) that take general human welfare into account but often forget the irreducibly singular human beings who constitute a political body. As I argued in the previous section, the obvious problem here is that the ethical obligations and responsibilities incurred in exposure do not necessarily arise from the Other human alone, for nonhuman animals and other nonhuman beings also have the potential to interrupt and oblige as well. Consequently, a posthumanist politics that begins from a thought of exposure must come to terms with responsibilities potentially arising from beyond the sphere of the human and must engage the possibility that existing forms of politics are unable to accommodate this enlarged scope of consideration.

It is only in recent years that posthumanist philosophers have begun to think through the question of the animal in this more inclusive manner. I would suggest that Agamben's early work was unable to proceed in this more inclusive manner primarily because, following thinkers such as Heidegger and Benveniste, he was working with an overly narrow interhuman and protolinguistic theory of the grounds of human subjectivity. At the same time, although his work was never explicitly *opposed* to an expanded notion of ethics and politics that would encompass nonhuman life, he failed to outline in a sufficient manner what form such an ethics and politics might take.

In a certain sense, then, Agamben's work *The Open* marks a rupture in the itinerary of his thought. If his thinking began primarily as a response to the nihilistic tendencies of humanism and human-based politics, his most recent work indicates that these concerns lead necessarily in some sense to directly addressing the larger issue of anthropocentrism that had previously been held in abeyance. And this direction is explicitly announced at the very outset of *The Open,* in the section entitled "Theriomorphous" (meaning, literally, having the form of an animal). Taking his point of departure from an illustration found in a thirteenth-century Hebrew Bible in the Ambrosian Library in Milan, which depicts the messianic banquet of the righteous on the last day, Agamben pauses to consider a curious detail about the portrait. The righteous represented in the illustration—who are enjoying their feast on the meat of the Leviathan and Behemoth with no concern for whether the slaughter was kosher, since they inhabit a space and time that is outside the law—are depicted as having *human* bodies and *animal* heads. "Why," Agamben wonders, "are the representatives of concluded humanity depicted with animal heads?" (O, 2).

Following certain interpretations of both the rabbinic and Talmudic traditions, Agamben suggests that the illustration can be read as announcing a double consequence encountered on the "last day" of humanity. He writes:

> It is not impossible . . . that in attributing an animal head to the remnant of Israel [that is, those who are remaining, the righteous who remain alive during the time of the Messiah's coming], the artist of the manuscript in the Ambrosian intended to suggest that on the last day, the relations between animals and men will take on a new form, and that man himself will be reconciled with his animal nature.
>
> (O, 3)

What we have here is an illustration representing two moments realized in the postapocalyptic time of the "end of man" and the "end of history." On the one hand—and this theme will be familiar to readers of Agamben's other writings—we encounter human beings who are reconciled with their animal natures and who no longer suffer the effects of the biopolitical separation of bare life and political life. To think through a human form-of-life that does not divide *zoē* from *bíos*—such would be the task of the politics of the coming community, a task and a politics that, as Agamben tells us, remain "largely to be invented."[14] On the other hand—and this is where a certain rupture can be marked in Agamben's own thought—we are given to think a transmutation in the relations *between human beings and animals,* where this difference is understood not simply as a division that occurs within human beings but rather as a differential relation between human beings, on the one hand, and so-called nonhuman animals, on the other. Although Agamben does not specify the precise dimensions of this transformed relation (any more than he specifies the exact form of the politics of the coming community), it is clear given the context that his reading of the illustration is pointing us toward a less violent conception of human-animal relations. Thus, just as Agamben's thought of the coming community is an effort to come to grips with and avert the political failures of our age, his reworking of the human-animal distinction appears to be aimed at creating a space in which human interactions with nonhuman life can take on a new form and economy that avoids similar disastrous consequences for nonhuman life. It will be useful to keep both of these prongs of Agamben's argument in mind as I turn to an investigation of the political and ontological obstacles blocking access to the realization of this kind of alternative mode of being-with other animals.

HUMANISM AND THE ANTHROPOLOGICAL MACHINE

Agamben gives the name "anthropological machine" (a concept he borrows from the Italian scholar of myth Furio Jesi) to the mechanism underlying our current means of determining the human-animal distinction. This machine can best be understood as the symbolic and material mechanisms at work in various scientific and philosophical discourses that classify and distinguish humans and animals through a dual process of inclusion and exclusion. The first chapters of *The Open* provide the reader with a fascinating overview of some of the historical variations on the anthropological machine at work in a number of authors and discourses, ranging from the philosophy of Georges Bataille and Alexandre Kojève to the taxonomic studies of Carl Linnaeus and post-Darwinian paleontology. For the purposes of the argument I am developing here, it will suffice to recall the general structure of the machine and why Agamben argues that it is necessary to stop its functioning.

Agamben makes a distinction between two key variations on the anthropological machine: the modern and premodern. The modern anthropological machine is post-Darwinian. It seeks to understand, following the principles of natural science, the emergence of the fully constituted human being from out of the order of the human animal (the latter, of course, is in many ways indistinguishable from certain nonhuman animals, especially so-called higher primates). In order to mark this transition, it is necessary to determine and isolate the animal aspects of the human animal and exclude them from humanity proper. Agamben describes this process as involving an "animalization" of certain modes of human life, an attempt to separate out—within human beings themselves—what precisely is animal, on the one hand, and human, on the other. This variation on the anthropological machine gives rise to the search by nineteenth-century paleontologists for the "missing link" that provides the biological transition from speechless ape to speaking human. But it also opens the way for the totalitarian and democratic experiments on and around human nature that function by excluding animal life from human life within human beings. Agamben suggests that "it is enough to move our field of research ahead a few decades, and instead of this innocuous paleontological find we will have the Jew, that is, the non-man produced within the man, or the *néomort* and the overcomatose person, that is, the animal separated within the human body itself" (O, 37).

The premodern form of the anthropological machine, which runs from Aristotle up through Linnaeus, functions in a similar but inverted form. Rather than animalizing certain aspects of the human, animal life is itself humanized. Human beings who take an essentially animal form are used to mark the constitutive outside of humanity proper: the infant savage, the wolf-man, the werewolf, the slave, or the barbarian. Here, the beings situated at the limits of humanity suffer similar consequences to those "animalized" beings caught within the working of the modern anthropological machine.

As Agamben suggests, the structure or machine that delimits the contours of the human is perfectly ironic and empty. It does not function by uncovering a uniquely human trait that demarcates a clean break between human and all other nonhuman animals—for, as Agamben himself acknowledges, no such trait or group of traits is to be found. This much we know from current debates in evolutionary biology and animal ethics. And here it is not so much a matter of subscribing to a watered-down, quasi-Darwinian continuism that would blur any and all distinctions one might wish to make between and among human and nonhuman animals but rather recognizing that deciding what constitutes "the human" and "the animal" is never simply a neutral scientific or ontological matter. Indeed, one of the chief merits of *The Open* is that it helps us to see that the locus and stakes of the human-animal distinction are almost always deeply *political and ethical.* For not only does the distinction create the opening for the exploitation of nonhuman animals and others considered not fully human (this is the point that is forcefully made by animal ethicists), but it also creates the conditions for contemporary biopolitics, in which more and more of the "biological" and "animal" aspects of human life are brought under the purview of the State and the juridical order.

As Agamben has argued in *Homo Sacer* and elsewhere, contemporary biopolitics, whether it manifests itself in totalitarian or democratic form, contains within it the virtual possibility of concentration camps and other violent means of producing and controlling bare life. It comes as no surprise, then, that he does not seek to articulate a more precise, more empirical, or less dogmatic determination of the human-animal distinction. Such a distinction would only redraw the lines of the "object" of biopolitics and further define the scope of its reach. Thus, instead of drawing a new human-animal distinction, Agamben insists that *the distinction must be abolished altogether,* and along with it the anthropological machine that produces the distinction. Recalling the political consequences that have followed from the modern and premodern separation of "human" and "animal" within human existence, Agamben characterizes the task for thought in the following terms: "it is not so much a matter of asking which of the two machines [i.e., the modern or premodern anthropological machine] . . . is better or more effective—or, rather, less lethal and bloody—as it is of understanding how they work so that we might, eventually, be able to stop them" (O, 38).

Now, the critic of Agamben's argument is likely to see a slippery-slope fallacy here. Why is it a *necessary* or even virtual possibility that every time a human-animal distinction is made that there will be negative ("lethal and bloody") political consequences for certain human beings? Isn't the promise of democratic humanism and Enlightenment modernism (the very traditions Agamben would have us leave behind) their foundational commitment to reform, their perfectibility and inclusiveness? Isn't it precisely humanism that guards against the worst excesses of totalitarianism and human rights abuses?

The reader who takes up a careful study of Agamben's work from this angle, seeking answers to such questions, will be well positioned to grasp its novelty. The overarching thesis of Agamben's work over the past decade is that there is in fact an "inner solidarity" between democracy and totalitarianism, not at an empirical level but at a historical and philosophical level.[15] Despite the enormous empirical differences between these two political systems, they are nevertheless united in their investment in the politics of the anthropological machine and in seeking to separate bare (animal) life from properly political (human) life. Even if democratic regimes maintain safeguards designed to prevent many of the totalitarian excesses perpetrated against bare life (and Agamben's references to Karen Quinlan and others make it clear that democracies are actually far from successful in such matters), they continue unwittingly to create the conditions of possibility for such consequences. This hidden implication of democracy comes to the fore especially in those instances where the rule of law is suspended, for example, in the declarations of sovereign exception to the law or in the refugee crisis that accompanies the decline of nation-states. Such states of exception are, Agamben argues (following Walter Benjamin), becoming more and more the rule in contemporary political life—and the examples one might adduce in support of this thesis are indeed becoming increasingly and troublingly commonplace. It is considerations of this kind that lead Agamben to the conclusion that the genuine political task facing us today is not the reform, radicalization, or expansion of humanism, democracy, and sovereignty, but creating an altogether different form of political life.

Agamben's work faces two important challenges at this level. On the one hand, neohumanists will (justifiably) wonder whether Agamben's "coming community" and rejection of the humanist tradition in favor of a nonsovereign and nonjuridical politics will be better able than current democracies to guard against the injustices he condemns. On the other hand, theorists of a more deconstructionist and Levinasian orientation will likely see Agamben's project as being constituted by a false dilemma between humanist democracy and a nonessentialist thought of community. Although such theorists would share Agamben's concerns about the problematic virtual possibilities of democratic politics and its ontology, they would be less sanguine about completely rejecting the democratic heritage. For them, the chief political task would consist in filtering through our democratic inheritance to unlock its radical possibilities, insisting on democracy's commitment to perfectibility so as to expand democracy's scope and to open democratic politics to its Other. This would bring democracy and its humanist commitments into relation with another thought of being-with Others that is similar to Agamben's coming community.

I should say that I find neither of these critical perspectives particularly persuasive and that I believe Agamben offers us overwhelmingly persuasive accounts of the limits of current forms of democracy and humanism. Furthermore, it should be noted that there are moments throughout his work where he gives instances of how his alternative thought of politics *can* be actualized in concrete circumstances. But even the most charitable reading of his work must acknowledge that in terms of the kinds of questions posed by neohumanists and deconstructionists, much remains to be worked out at both the theoretical and concrete political level in Agamben's project. And if the scope of this discussion were limited to an anthropocentric politics, I would argue that the questions and criticisms raised by neohumanists and deconstructionists are very difficult to circumvent. Humanism, democracy, and human rights are complicated and rich historical constructs, with the intrinsic potential for extensive and remarkably progressive reforms.

And yet, if *the question of the animal* were taken seriously here and the political discussion were moved to that level as well, the stakes of the debate would change considerably. Who among those activists and theorists working in defense of animals seriously believes that humanism, democracy, and human rights are the sine qua non of ethics and politics? Even those theorists who employ the logic of these discourses in an extensionist manner so as to bring animals within the sphere of moral and political considerability do not seem to believe that an ethics and a politics that genuinely respect animal life can be accomplished within the confines of the traditions they use.

On this political terrain, neohumanist arguments concerning the merits of the democratic tradition have little if any weight. Even if one were to inscribe animal rights within a democratic liberatory narrative of expansion and perfectibility (as is sometimes done), such gestures can only appear tragicomic in light of the massive institutionalized abuse of animals that contemporary democracies not only tolerate but encourage on a daily basis. And in many democracies, the support of animal abuse goes much further. Currently, militant animal activists in the United States who engage in economic sabotage and property destruction in the name of stopping the worst forms of animal abuse are not just criticized (and in many cases without sound justification) but are placed at the top of the list of "domestic terrorists" by the F.B.I. and subject to outrageously unjust penalties and prison sentences. In view of the magnitude of such problems, animal activists are currently embroiled in a protracted debate over the merits of a reformist (welfarist) versus a stricter and more radical rightist (incrementalist) approach to animal issues and over which approach is more effective in the contemporary political and legal contexts. However, the real question seems to me to lie elsewhere—precisely in the decision to be made between the project of radicalizing existing politics to accommodate nonhuman life (an expansion of neohumanism and deconstruction) and that of working toward the kind of coming politics advocated by Agamben that would allow for an entirely new economy of human-animal relations. While Agamben's thought is sometimes pejoratively labeled by critics as utopian inasmuch as it seeks a complete change in our political thinking and practices without offering the concrete means of achieving such change, from the perspective of the question of the animal, the tables can easily be turned on the critics. Anyone who argues that existing forms of politics can be reformed or radicalized so as to do justice to the multiplicity of forms of nonhuman life is clearly the unrealistic and utopian thinker, for what signs or sources of hope do we have that humanism and democracy (both of which are grounded in an agent-centered conception of subjectivity) can be radicalized or reformed so as to include and give direct consideration to beings beyond the human?[16]

Thus, when we consider the ethicopolitical status of animal life, the necessity for working toward a form of politics beyond the present humanist, democratic, and juridical orders becomes clear. Even Jacques Derrida—who, as I shall show in the following chapter, has always taken a nuanced and generally respectful stance toward humanism and the law, refusing either fully to endorse or reject them—has acknowledged the limits of legislation in this regard. Concerning political and ethical relations between human beings and animals, he argues:

> A transformation is . . . necessary and inevitable, for reasons that are both conscious and unconscious. Slow, laborious, sometimes gradual, sometimes accelerated, the mutation of relations between humans and animals will not necessarily or solely take the form of a charter, a declaration of rights, or a tribunal governed by a legislator. I do not believe in the miracle of legislation. Besides, there is already a law, more or less empirical, and that's better than nothing. But it does not prevent the slaughtering, or the "techno-scientific" pathologies of the market or of industrial production.[17]

The point that I wish to make here is that were sufficient attention given to the question of the animal by Agamben, his arguments aimed at the limitations of the logic of sovereignty and our current political and juridical models would become *significantly* more powerful and persuasive. That Agamben chooses to avoid this approach is indicative of a kind of performative anthropocentrism in his texts. In what follows, I argue that if Agamben and other posthumanist approaches to politics are unable overcome this kind of anthropocentrism, the logic of the anthropological machine will reassert itself in places where we least expect it.

Let us return, then, to Agamben's main question: How best to halt the anthropological machine and create a posthumanist politics that is no longer governed by its "lethal and bloody" logic?

One of Agamben's key theses in *The Open* is that Heidegger's thinking—despite its uncompromisingly critical relation to humanism—does little more than replicate the inner logic of the anthropological machine. The majority of the second half of *The Open* is taken up with a lengthy and intricate reading of Heidegger, in which Agamben attempts to demonstrate how Heidegger's scattered remarks on the difference between human Dasein and animal life implicitly obeys the inclusionary-exclusionary logic of the anthropological machine. Focusing primarily on Heidegger's *Fundamental Concepts of Metaphysics* and *Parmenides* lecture courses, Agamben's reading of these texts stresses the *proximity* of human Dasein with animal life, as well as the essential continuity that binds human and animal in their shared "captivation" by beings in their respective environments. As Agamben understands Heidegger's thought, human Dasein differs from its animal Other only by the very smallest of differences. What allows human Dasein to emerge in its singularity, along with the world relation and political possibilities concomitant with the emergence of Dasein, is simply that human animals have the unique capacity to grasp, or catch sight of, their being-captivated, a possibility that is (presumably) blocked off for animal life:

> Man, in the experience of profound boredom, has risked himself in the suspension of his relationship with the environment as a living being. . . . [He is able] to remember captivation an instant before a world disclosed itself. . . . Dasein is simply an animal that has learned to become bored; it has awakened *from* its own captivation *to* its own captivation. This awakening of the living being to its own being-captivated, this anxious and resolute opening to a not-open, is the human. (*O*, 70)

In this "brief instant" before world opens, in the moment at which the human animal awakens *from* its captivation *to* its captivation, human Dasein is thrust into the "space" or opening of the ontological difference. This is a topos that, while typically hidden, comes explicitly to the fore in certain moods such as anxiety and boredom, moods where the tight grip of captivation that binds a human being to other beings in its world gives way to the malaise and uncanniness of the indifference of other beings.

Inasmuch as Heidegger's account of the emergence of human Dasein is predicated on the capture and exclusion of the animal's particular mode of relation (namely, *Benommenheit,* captivation) to other beings, Agamben suggests that his thinking follows in lockstep with the logic of the anthropological machine. And Heidegger's political writings—especially the texts of the early to mid-1930s—provides an even clearer example of how the anthropological machine is at play throughout his writings, inasmuch as Heidegger there seeks to "ground" political life in the unique world relation of human Dasein, a world that is explicitly contrasted with the "worldless" realm of animal life in *An Introduction to Metaphysics.*

It is arguable whether Heidegger ever gave up the aim of uncovering a new political or historical task for human beings. *If* he did in fact recognize the error of doing so along nationalistic lines, it is unclear whether he gave up hope in uncovering some other "ground" for reorienting human existence. At the very least, we *can* be certain that Heidegger's thinking remains beholden to the logic of the anthropological machine from beginning to end. Heidegger never renounces the task of determining the proper of the human (as Da-sein, as ek-sistence), or the task of thinking through the redemption of Being (that is, the letting be of beings in their Being) that would occur were this human propriety to be assumed as such.

Heidegger's inability to think the relation between human and non-human life beyond or outside the logic of anthropological machine is what leads Agamben to look elsewhere for an alternative thought of the political. Not surprisingly—for this is a common gesture in his work—he finds his inspiration in Walter Benjamin's writings. Agamben is particularly interested in Benjamin's notions of the "saved night" (O, 81–82) and the "dialectic at a standstill," (O, 83) inasmuch as both notions offer an alternative image of the relation between nature and the human that does not rely on a rigid conceptual separation of the two realms. Such concepts seem to offer an idea of the human and the animal that places the anthropological machine "completely out of play" (O, 81). For Benjamin, the "saved night" refers to a natural world that is sufficient in itself, a world that has value independent of the role it might play as a dwelling place for human beings or as the stage where human history is acted out. When the natural world is viewed as having inherent value as it is in itself—as irreparable and unsavable, as not in need of being redeemed by human beings or serving human ends—the dialectic between human and animal comes to a "standstill." On Agamben's reading, Benjamin seeks this standstill not because he is concerned with articulating another, more refined instance of the human-animal distinction but rather because he seeks to abandon such conceptual work altogether. In the final analysis, Benjamin's texts leave the so-called human and nonhuman to be *as they are,* that is, in their singular, irreparable manner. Such letting-be has no need, as it does in Heidegger, of passing through human *logos* or history in order to come to presence. Rather, Benjamin's thought proposes for us the possibility of letting beings be *outside of being*.

It should come as no surprise that these Benjaminian themes provide the impetus and direction for Agamben's reading of Western history as the unfolding and vicissitudes of the anthropological machine. Benjamin's thought provides Agamben with the possibility of thinking about human beings and the nonhuman world beyond the dominant logic and terms provided by the Western metaphysical tradition. And the overarching task of *The Open*, at least as I have tried to argue here, is precisely to open up this possibility. In brief, Agamben's task is to provide readers with a philosophical concept, that is, with a conceptual monkey wrench that can be used to jam the anthropological machine—a machine that serves as the seemingly unsurpassable political and ontological horizon of our time. Agamben's notions of human and animal life as "unsavable" or "irreparable" are just such concepts. They are meant to provide readers with a glimpse of a world not subject to strictly anthropocentric aims or the "hyperbolic naïveté"[18] of modern humanity and its human chauvinism. As Agamben suggests in *The Coming Community*, affirming life in its irreparableness and profanity is a form of Nietzschean life affirmation. In this sense, the concept of unsavable life is offered as one way among others of assuming Zarathustra's task of remaining "true to the earth" and its inhabitants.

Agamben himself admits that trying to think about a humanity that is absolutely exposed and irreparable is not an easy task (O, 90). Indeed, one could read the whole of his work as a series of efforts to articulate this one thought: what form such an irreparable humanity, and a politics befitting such a humanity, might take. Reading Agamben from this perspective would also provide insight into the critical texts in which he probes the dangers and limitations of existing models of biopolitics and sovereignty. Our current models of politics are all, in one way or another, beholden to an image of humanity that is predicated on excluding our irreparableness. The task for thought, then, would be to highlight this limitation and to offer another, more affirmative and compelling concept and practice in its place.

With regard to human politics, Agamben seems to realize that such a concept is not to be achieved "all in one go." Given the ubiquity of the anthropological machine in both symbolic and material structures, the critical and deconstructive gesture of jamming the anthropological machine is just as important as the positive project of articulating another nonbinary and nonhierarchical concept of the human. With regard to rethinking *animal* life, the task is fraught with *far more severe difficulties,* if only for the simple fact that most of the theorists and philosophers working in this area have paid scant attention to the question of the animal. As I argued above, Agamben's writings are no exception here, as they focus entirely and exclusively on the effects of the anthropological machine *on human beings* and never explore the impact the machine has on various forms of animal life. Surely the latter type of analysis is needed if we are to begin to develop another mode of relation and community with nonhuman life. Such a project, as humble and painstaking as it is, perhaps lacks the pathos characteristic of the sharp rupture with previous political structures hinted at in Agamben's messianic politics, but it is every bit as necessary if we wish to develop a notion of community that truly avoids the "lethal and bloody" logic of the anthropological machine. In the following chapter, I turn to the writings of Jacques Derrida for further assistance in thinking through the ontological, ethical, and political dimensions of such a project.

CHAPTER FOUR

The Passion of the Animal

Derrida

And once again we are back to the question of the animal.
—JACQUES DERRIDA

INTRODUCTION

In 1997, some thirty years after the publication of his first three major works, Jacques Derrida made the following statement:

> The question of the living and of the living animal . . . will always have been the most important and decisive question. I have addressed it a thousand times, either directly or obliquely, by means of readings of *all* the philosophers I have taken an interest in.[1]

This statement will likely appear odd both to longtime readers of Derrida and to those readers who are familiar with debates in animal philosophy. While Derrida's name and work have, in recent years, been generally aligned with progressive political discourses and movements, only rarely has the importance of his thought been recognized for issues concerning animals. Indeed, among the literally tens of thousands of studies on Derrida published in the past three decades, the number of pieces devoted solely to the question of the animal in his work can be counted on ten, perhaps fewer, fingers. How to account for this disparity? Is Derrida's statement about the decisive importance of the question of life and the animal mere hyperbole? If it is not, how are we to explain the utter dearth of writings on this theme by his followers and critics? It would be tempting to explain the disparity away by saying that Derrida did not write explicitly or at length on animals until the mid-1980s, a time that coincides with the so-called ethicopolitical turn in his work. But as tempting as this explanation might be—and it is not completely lacking in justification—it does not square at all with Derrida's own remarks in the same 1997 essay, in which he says that the issue of animals has been his concern all along and that he has been making "arguments of a theoretical or philosophical kind, or in what we can call a deconstructive style," with regard to the question of the animal for a very long time, "since [he] began writing in fact" (AIA, 402).

While Derrida's readers can perhaps be forgiven for being caught off guard with respect to the importance of the question of the animal in his work, it is not difficult to demonstrate that this question is in fact important and decisive throughout his vast oeuvre. From the very earliest to the latest texts, Derrida is keenly aware of and intent on problematizing the anthropocentric underpinnings and orientation of philosophy and associated discourses. This project takes place across a number of fronts and through various modes of intervention. The most constant aspect of Derrida's concern with the question of the animal is evident in his efforts to underscore the anthropocentric dimensions of ontotheological humanism. He develops this critical point primarily in view of Heidegger's deconstructive engagement with the tradition, which Heidegger interrogates from the perspective of the role that presence and self-presence play in the determination of the being of the human. If the main stakes for Heidegger in his critical confrontation with ontotheological humanism revolve around a rethinking of the being of the human and its role in determining the Being of beings, it is not at all clear that Derrida shares this focus on the human. For not only does he cast a suspicious glance on the idea that there is anything "proper" (that is to say, essential in an exclusive and binary sense) to human beings (a claim that Heidegger is wont to make, as we have seen), but he also interrogates the manner in which the logic of the proper functions to draw a simple and reductive dividing line between human and animal. Thus we find in *Of Grammatology* the claim that the term "human" gains sense only in relation to a series of excluded terms and identities, foremost among them nature and animality.[2] Similarly, in *Glas*, Derrida underscores the point that the ontotheological philosophical tradition is fundamentally humanist and anthropocentric and that this tradition has as yet been unable to come to grips with the "second blow" to human narcissism that Darwin delivered in undercutting the religious foundations of classical forms of the human-animal distinction.[3] Derrida also finds traces of this religious humanism and anthropocentrism even among the very best critics of the tradition, such as Walter Benjamin[4] and Emmanuel Levinas. In Derrida's 1964 essay on Levinas, for example, he takes Levinas's thought of the face to task for its reliance upon anthropocentric and religious notions of the ethical and the human and for its unwitting use of a simple and simplistic human-animal distinction.[5]

The latter point, concerning a reductive understanding of the human-animal distinction, is one of the invariable themes in Derrida's writings concerning the question of the animal. Here Derrida is at pains to argue that binary oppositions between human beings and animals are not only empirically inaccurate but also overlook the various differences we find between and among human beings themselves and animals themselves. The vast majority of what Derrida has written on the issue of animals and animality touches on the abundant ways in which philosophers and theorists have tried to cleanly and clearly separate human beings from animals using single traits, characteristics, or (to use Derrida's language) "propers." Entire essays and chapters of books have been devoted to a deconstruction of traits or capacities often thought to be uniquely human such as "the hand,"[6] spirit,[7] nudity,[8] and awareness of death,[9] while other traits such as language, reason, responsibility, and technology are discussed critically only in passing. Throughout these texts, it is clear that Derrida is highly suspicious of classical formulations of the human-animal distinction and is seeking to rethink differences between human beings and animals in a nonhierarchical and nonbinary way. I will examine this issue in considerable detail in the following two sections of this chapter.

Beyond the critical tasks of calling attention to the anthropocentric aspects of ontotheological humanism and questioning its reliance on binary oppositions in thinking about differences between and among human beings and animals, Derrida's work also gestures toward the positive project of trying to think otherwise about animal life and its place in ethics and politics. This positive project is, like much else in Derrida's work that is aimed at articulating an alternative to the traditions he inherits and deconstructs, not as fully worked out as his critical and negative projects; nevertheless, there is a significant amount of material devoted to this task that is relevant to tracking the question of the animal in his work. Along these lines, there are two major strategies that Derrida employs. The first is to develop a series of "infrastructures" (such as "*dif-férance*," supplement, arche-writing, etc.) that are not exclusively human. Although Derrida has always insisted that such notions as "*différance*," the trace, ex-appropriation, and so forth circulate and function well beyond humanity,[10] many of his best and most loyal readers have missed this aspect of his thought. What Derrida seems most interested in developing with these sorts of quasi concepts and infrastructures is not just a decentering of human subjectivity (as is sometimes supposed) but rather a thought of the Same-Other relation where the Same is not simply a *human* self and where the Other is not simply a *human* other. At bottom, what these infrastructures seek to give for thought is a notion of *life as responsivity*, where life is understood not exclusively but broadly and inclusively, ranging from human to animal and beyond. Stated in very bald terms, Derrida thesis here seems to be that wherever among life forms we find something like an identity, there the play of difference, affect, inheritance, response, and so on will be at work. From this perspective, there is no clear separation between human and animal inasmuch as both "kinds" of beings are irreducibly caught up in the "same" network of differential forces that constitute their modes of existence.

The second chief strategy that Derrida's positive project employs is to bring animals within the scope of ethical and political considerations. If one of the overarching dogmatisms of the ontotheological philosophical tradition has been that animals are incapable of ethics and politics and thus fall outside the scope of ethical and political concern, then one of the main advances of Derrida's thought is his attempt to develop an idea of ethics and politics that avoids repeating these standard theses. Here again it is clear that the major political motifs and infrastructures of his work from the mid-1980s forward (democracy to come, the gift, hospitality, friendship without friendship, the messianic, and so forth) are not intended to exclude animals from their scope. Indeed, not only does Derrida explicitly extend these infrastructures to include animals, thus bringing them within the scope of ethics and politics, he also insists that animals have the capacity to interrupt one's existence and inaugurate ethical and political encounters. In this vein, he discusses at length the violence and injustices suffered by animals[11] and, in contrast to Levinas in particular, makes it clear that animals confront us with as much ethical force as human beings do, if not more.[12]

This thumbnail sketch of the broad range of themes and questions concerning animals in Derrida's work should, I hope, go some way toward supporting Derrida's claim that the question of life and the animal has been "the most important and decisive" question for him all along and also give some credence to the notion that in his work this theme is a guiding thread that is worth tracking and trying to understand.[13] For the moment, I will leave this taxonomy of animal texts and themes to one side and turn to the project of trying to elaborate a more rigorous and more general account of what is at stake in Derrida's work on the question of the animal. Anyone who has read Derrida with some care will know that such a gesture is inherently problematic, for all of his writings are deeply context-dependent and text-specific. And yet without something like a general account in place, the import of the question of the animal in his work will go (as it has to date) largely unnoticed. As such, I offer the following remarks as a means of gaining access to Derrida's work on this issue and also with an eye toward assessing the philosophical and political dimensions of his thought.

The approach I am taking here has other limitations that should be noted. On the one hand, I will not be able to take into account the specific interventions in the work of major thinkers that comprise the bulk of Derrida's texts on animals from the mid-1980s to the late 1990s. Although most of the thinkers that he engages during this period, viz., Heidegger, Levinas, Lacan, Aristotle, Descartes, and Kant, figure directly or indirectly in this chapter, it is worth noting that the texts devoted to these thinkers each focus on a singular textual site and configuration of themes that need to be attended to in their specificity should the reader wish to grasp the overarching stakes of those essays. Likewise, Derrida has numerous texts that employ animal figures, imagery, and metaphors (for example, hedgehogs, animal-machines, chimeras), and each essay uses these animal figures for different ends. An analysis of these texts from the point of view of the question of the animal would certainly be worthwhile, but it falls outside the scope of the present chapter. Again, in avoiding these aspects of his work, I certainly am not intending to downplay their significance. Rather, my aim is to move directly to the theoretical stakes of Derrida's work on the question of the animal so that these other dimensions will be more easily understood. Furthermore, a general theoretical account will allow me to address what I take to be the chief limitations and advances in Derrida's approach to the question of the animal.

With those caveats in mind, I shall argue in what follows that Derrida's work on animals consists of three main aspects: (1) A kind of "proto-ethical" imperative that gives rise to (2) a concrete ethicopolitical position, on the one hand, and (3) a thorough reworking of the basic anthropocentric thrust of the Western philosophical tradition, on the other hand. The most complicated and intricate aspects of Derrida's thought, and the ones that require the most exposition and patience to understand, concern the proto-ethical imperative (point 1) that grounds this project along with the texts devoted to reworking of the ontological and philosophical tradition (point 3). Consequently, it will be easier to approach these more difficult ideas if I can first lay out Derrida's general ethicopolitical position and then see how this basic position informs and is informed by the more complicated aspects of his project.

ANIMAL VIOLENCE

Theorists in Anglo-American philosophical and legal debates concerning the status and well-being of animals usually employ either a sentience-based utilitarian approach or a subject-based rights approach in their work. Derrida's writings make use of aspects of both of these approaches but also depart from them in important ways. In line with most pro-animal theorists and activists, Derrida is strongly opposed to the violence and injustice suffered by billions of animals in contemporary society. His objection to the mistreatment of these animals appeals to their sentience (the central aspect of the utilitarian position), while his support for the long-term transformation of this situation is couched in terms of maximum respect (the key notion of rights-based animal ethics) for animals and a sympathy and strategic support for the animal rights movement. Derrida's most explicit account of his position on these matters is found in the presentation of one of his "hypotheses" on the question of the animal in his essay "The Animal That Therefore I Am." There he writes of an unprecedented transformation in the treatment of and thinking about animals over the last two centuries that has occurred along two lines: increased subjection of animals, and more compassion toward them. He links the increased subjection and violent treatment of animals with scientific and technological developments in the rearing, slaughtering, and use of animals for the betterment of human welfare.

This point about the increased and violent subjection of animals is an essential one and worth underscoring, for Derrida is one of the very few prominent philosophers in the Continental tradition not just to allude to this violence but to name and examine it with care.[14] Although human violence toward animals is certainly nothing historically novel, Derrida is correct to remark that over the past two centuries (and in the past century in particular) violence toward animals has increased and accelerated at an exponential rate. During this recent period, he notes that

> traditional forms of treatment of the animal have been turned upside down by the joint developments of zoological, ethological, biological, and genetic *forms of knowledge* and the always inseparable *techniques* of intervention with respect to their object, the transformation of the actual object, its milieu, its world, namely, the living animal. This has occurred by means of farming and regimentalization at a demographic level unknown in the past, by means of genetic experimentation, the industrialization of what can be called the production for consumption of animal meat, artificial insemination on a massive scale, more and more audacious manipulations of the genome, the reduction of the animal not only to production and overactive reproduction (hormones, genetic crossbreeding, cloning, and so on) of meat for consumption but also of all sorts of other end products, and all of that in the service of a certain being and the so-called human well-being of man. *(AIA, 394)*

This passage requires little commentary along empirical lines, for these facts can certainly be verified (although not without considerable effort, as much of the relevant information surrounding the treatment of animals is not always readily available). Much more could be said, though, in terms of the causal factors behind this massive shift: what, besides the development of science and technology, has been the driving force behind this increased subjection of animals? Economic forces? Human chauvinism? Exponential population growth? Widespread ethicopolitical insensitivity?

Derrida is profoundly concerned with this question, as are a number of theorists in other philosophical traditions and in other disciplines beyond philosophy. But before addressing this issue, we should pause for a moment to consider why this increased violence toward animals has not been more of a question for thought in recent Continental philosophy, the context in which Derrida writes and is most often read. Whatever one might make of the so-called analytic-Continental split, it is generally agreed that Continental philosophers place a priority on concrete existential and ethicopolitical issues over abstract metaphysical and epistemological issues. In other words, even when Continental philosophers turn to ontology and epistemology, it is typically ethicopolitical matters that inform this turn. Thus, in reading such philosophers as Jürgen Habermas, Gianni Vattimo, Emmanuel Levinas, Jean-François Lyotard, Giorgio Agamben, or Phillipe Lacoue-Labarthe, one can readily recognize that, at bottom, their work proceeds in response to one or another of the ethical and political questions of our century. Given the European site of Continental philosophy, the Nazi Holocaust is a common and privileged referent for many of these thinkers. In view of the scope and consequences of the Nazi Holocaust, giving even minor attention to the mistreatment of animals in this political and philosophical context might appear at first blush to be highly questionable, and to dare to equate or compare the Nazi Holocaust with the mistreatment of animals would seem to be even more questionable. When Heidegger risked this comparison in his infamous "mechanized food industry" remark, one of his most careful readers, Lacoue-Labarthe, called the comparison "scandalously inadequate,"[15] and I believe that, in Heidegger's case at least, such a judgment is correct (which is to say, in regard to Heidegger's thought the comparison is scandalously inadequate because of his subsequent silence about the Nazi Holocaust, especially in view of his own support of Nazism). But unless we are willing to beg the question at hand, we cannot view the comparison of violence toward human beings and animals as scandalously inadequate *simply* because it compares human to nonhuman life (which, it would seem, is one of Lacoue-Labarthe's main points of contention with Heidegger's remark). What the question of the animal obliges us to consider is precisely the anthropocentric value hierarchy that places human life always and everywhere in a higher rank over animal life. Such a value hierarchy seems to be presupposed by nearly every major thinker in recent Continental thought—and this despite the fact of the continuing rise and widespread presence of animal rights discourse in both philosophy and society at large.

Perhaps the issue of violence toward animals can provoke thought in this philosophical context *only* if it is compared with the worst forms of interhuman violence. Derrida briefly discusses the comparison of human and animal genocides in order to pose precisely this question. In recent years, several prominent animal rights groups have risked comparing current methods of animal rearing and slaughtering with the Nazi Holocaust, a strategy that has been met with mixed responses and mixed results, and, closer to the context of Continental thought, several prominent authors and philosophers, including Isaac Singer and Theodor Adorno,[16] have made the same comparison and drawn analogies between misanthropy and hatred of animals. Here, too, such proposals have been met with mixed responses. Comparisons and analogies between the treatment of human beings in concentration camps and animals in factory farms are, of course, always open to the charge of being false analogies inasmuch as there are significant and irreducible differences between factory farms and concentration camps and between the historical, social, and economic forces behind the abuse and murder of human beings and violence toward animals. But the most common manner of dismissing these analogies is to reject *any* comparison between interhuman and interspecies violence on the grounds that such comparisons denigrate human suffering. Most religious and secular forms of humanism would have us believe a priori that human life has more value and moral weight than animal life and that it is precisely because of this value difference that any comparison between human and animal genocide is objectionable.[17]

As I mentioned above, Derrida's work is aimed at undercutting these kinds of value hierarchies, and, as a result, he is not as quick to dismiss the comparison of human and animal genocide on humanist grounds as other theorists have been. In addition to acknowledging that literal animal genocides have occurred and are still under way ("there are also animal genocides: the number of species endangered because of man takes one's breath away" [*AIA*, 394]), Derrida points out that many of the analogies that are drawn between human and animal genocide overlook the singular situation and suffering of *animals*. In so doing, he implicitly contests the humanist notion that comparisons between human and animal suffering are objectionable because human beings are supposed to carry more inherent value. Following Derrida, one might reject, or at least wish to complicate, the analogizing of human and animal genocides not simply to salvage human chauvinism but rather to attend to the specificity and singularity of the situation of *animals*. It is with this aim in mind that Derrida will

> neither abuse the figure of genocide nor consider it explained away. For it gets more complicated here: the annihilation of certain species is indeed in process, but it is occurring through the organization and exploitation of an artificial, infernal, virtually interminable survival, in conditions that previous generations would have judged monstrous, outside of every supposed norm of a life proper to animals that are thus exterminated by means of their continued existence or even their overpopulation. As if, for example, instead of throwing people into ovens or gas chambers (let's say Nazi) doctors and geneticists had decided to organize the overproduction and overgeneration of Jews, gypsies, and homosexuals by means of artificial insemination, so that, being more numerous and better fed, they could be destined in always increasing numbers for the same hell, that of the imposition of genetic experimentation or extermination by gas or by fire. In the same abattoirs. (AIA, 395)

Derrida's position here—that one should neither abuse nor considered explained away the figure of genocide when extended to animals—is, I think, defensible and well considered. Comparisons of human and animal suffering can sometimes be abused when they are employed in a facile, thoughtless, and offensive manner. But, at the same time, not all such comparisons should be dismissed a priori on the grounds that human suffering is always and everywhere more important and of more value than animal suffering. The very difficult task for thought here is to bear the burden of thinking through both kinds of suffering in their respective singularity *and* to notice relevant similarities and parallel logics at work where they exist. To do so requires abandoning, or at least inhabiting in a hypercritical manner, the hierarchical humanist metaphysics that we have inherited from the ontotheological tradition, for it is this tradition that blocks the possibility of thinking about animals in a non- or other-than-anthropocentric manner.

In the same "hypothesis" we have been discussing concerning animal subjection—the hypothesis that in the past two centuries there has been an unprecedented and exponential increase in violence toward animals—Derrida ventures a related proposition about another recent change in human-animal relations. Along with an exponential increase in violence against animals, he calls attention to the concomitant increase in the presence and force of the so-called animal protection movement. He describes this alternative force, which is itself not utterly free of violence toward animals (a point to which I shall return below), as comprising "minority, weak, marginal voices, little assured of their discourse, of their right to discourse and of the enactment of their discourse within the law," voices whose aim is "to awaken us to our responsibilities and our obligations with respect to the living in general" (*AIA*, 395). He sees these two forces—that of the massive, industrialized, and intensive modes of violence against animals, on the one hand, and that of the counterforce of animal protection on the other—as engaged in a protracted struggle over the extent of pity and compassion toward animals. There is no doubt for Derrida that this is an "unequal" struggle, with the animal protection and animal rights movements being the minority force in the struggle. But the question that he offers for consideration, the overarching "hypothesis" he offers in regard to the struggle between the force of violence and the counterforce of the animal protection movement, is that regardless of the inequality and overdetermined nature of this struggle, we are nevertheless living through a moment where this struggle has become, to use a Derridean turn of phrase, *incontournable,* uncircumventable for thought. The question of violence and compassion toward animals has, in a certain sense, become one of the leading questions of our age. The war between violence and compassion is thus

> passing through a critical phase. We are passing through that phase and it passes through us. To think the war we find ourselves waging is not only a duty, a responsibility, and obligation, it is also a necessity, a constraint that, like it or not, directly or indirectly, everyone is held to. Henceforth and more than ever. And I say "to think" this war, because it concerns what we call "thinking."   (*AIA*, 397)

The reference to "thinking" here indicates that this question is situated at the limits of philosophy and the metaphysical tradition and that the resources to think through this question are not likely to be found wholly within that tradition. Whether the animal protection and animal rights movements provide a successful and sustainable alternative thought and practice in regard to animals, one that offers a fundamental challenge to metaphysical anthropocentrism, is one of the questions around which we can begin to articulate Derrida's position in relation to existing discourses in animal ethics.

I suggested at the outset of this chapter that Derrida's writings on animals contain a positive ethicopolitical dimension. How, precisely, does this aspect of Derrida's work relate to existing debates in the field of animal ethics? Although Derrida does not specifically mention the work of such philosophers as Peter Singer and Tom Regan, it is clear that he is in agreement with the general goals of the animal liberation and animal rights movements. In an interview with Elizabeth Roudinesco,[18] Derrida explicitly states his opposition to a whole host of practices that involve the mistreatment and killing of animals, including factory farming, industrialized slaughter, purely instrumental forms of experimentation, and bullfighting, and he openly and forcefully criticizes many of the standard arguments against vegetarianism, including the oft-raised arguments from nutritional deficiency (vegetarian diets are nutritionally deficient), culinary tradition (animal flesh is essential to the maintenance of our respected culinary tradition), and interanimal violence (since animals kill and eat one another, why shouldn't we?). In addition, he explicitly states his general sympathy and solidarity with the animal rights movement in this interview and in other places in his writing. To be sure, Derrida's discourse on the concrete ethical and political stakes of animal rights is nowhere near as refined as the arguments and positions outlined by Singer and Regan and other thinkers in Anglo-American philosophy. But, I think it is safe to say that his position overlaps substantially and in important ways with the main aims of rights-based and sentience-based animal ethics, whatever the theoretical and ethical differences between these two approaches (and there are many).

My suspicion is that many of Derrida's more philosophically inclined readers get frustrated at this point with his work. Why does he not go on to outline a concrete political platform and provide a rigorous ethical theory as a ground for this platform? Besides the problem with seeing theory as informing practice in any straightforward manner (for Derrida, the relation between ethics and politics is irreducibly aporetic), it is important to understand that Derrida's work is primarily aimed at *calling into question* the dominant avenues through which one might seek to effect change. Despite his sympathy for the animal rights and animal liberation movements, he remains deeply skeptical of the notion that *fundamental* changes in our thinking and relation with animals can be effected through existing ethical and political discourses and institutions. Deconstruction is situated precisely at this level, namely, at the level of trying to articulate another thought of relation (ethics) and practice (politics) that moves beyond the limits of anthropocentric traditions and institutions. This task requires a considerable amount of invention as well as time. This does *not* mean, of course, that Derrida is a fatalist with regard to the present circumstances under which animals live and die. He supports and sympathizes with the animal rights movement precisely because it is engaged in trying to limit violence toward animals to the greatest extent possible. But he departs from dominant forms of animal rights discourse and practice inasmuch as he believes that a fundamental transformation of human-animal relations requires a deconstruction of the very notion of moral and legal rights and its underlying metaphysical and philosophical support.

Thus, with respect to existing institutions and present-day activism and interventionist strategies, Derrida advocates a contextual or situational ethics and politics that are aligned with animal rights. Ethics and politics would be a matter of acting and making decisions in concrete circumstances, using as much knowledge as possible, and in view of a "maximum respect" (*VA*, 73) for animals. He offers no overarching program of action but rather suggests that a "slow and progressive approach" (*VA*, 74) to the elimination of violence against animals is necessary. Derrida does not, to my knowledge, ever wade into the debates over welfarism and abolitionism in terms of activist strategies, but given his various remarks on real-world animal rights politics, the position he advocates is perhaps closest to the incremental abolitionism advocated by legal theorist and activist Gary Francione.[19] Of course, given Derrida's ethical situationalism, it is entirely possible that he would have personally endorsed reforming (rather than abolishing) a specific violent practice (e.g., invasive medical experimentation) in a given political circumstance. In the final analysis, his work remains (no doubt intentionally) ambiguous on the question of general strategies in the field of animal rights.

I suggested earlier that Derrida's writings on animals are guided by a "proto-ethical" imperative of sorts and that this imperative gives rise to a concrete position in the field of animal rights as well as a contestation of philosophical anthropocentrism. Up to this point, I have outlined the basic aspects of Derrida's concrete ethicopolitical position in view of existing debates in Anglo-American animal ethics. In order to gain a fuller picture of Derrida's thought on the question of the animal, it will also be necessary to examine the proto-ethical imperative underlying his work as well his confrontation with anthropocentrism. As I mentioned earlier, and the reader should keep this in mind when working through the next two sections, these two areas of his work are considerably more complicated than the situationalist ethics and politics I have examined thus far.

Derrida's most explicit and sustained account of the proto-ethical imperative that figures in his writings on animals is found in his discussion of Jeremy Bentham in "The Animal That Therefore I Am." As is well known, in his *Introduction to the Principles of Morals and Legislation,* Bentham laments the fact that animals are treated as mere things, and he states his grief over the fact that a great portion of humanity receives the same poor and unthinking treatment as animals.[20] For Bentham, there can be no rigorous justification for ignoring the suffering of either human beings or animals, and his hope is that one day such injustices will be transformed:

> The day may come, when the rest of the animal creation may acquire those rights which never could have been withholden from them but by the hand of tyranny. The French have already discovered that the blackness of skin is no reason why a human being should be abandoned without redress to the caprice of a tormentor. It may come one day to be recognized, that the number of legs, the villosity of the skin, or the termination of the *os sacrum,* are reasons equally insufficient for abandoning a sensitive being to the same fate. What else is it that should trace the insuperable line? Is it the faculty of reason, or perhaps, the faculty for discourse? . . . The question is not, Can they *reason?* nor, Can they *talk?* but, Can they *suffer?*[21]

Peter Singer takes this passage as one of his central inspirations in *Animal Liberation*, pressing Bentham's consequentialist, sentience-based hedonic utilitarianism into the service of his own form of preference utilitarianism. His argument revolves around the interests and preferences animals have in not being subjected to suffering. As for Bentham, the primary ethical issue for Singer is not whether animals have a variety of human characteristics (reason, the capacity for speech, etc.), for the presence or absence of these traits is irrelevant to the simple fact that suffering and the frustration of preferences in sentient beings are the primary factors that guide moral decision making. Within a utilitarian framework of the sort advanced by both Bentham and Singer, animal suffering must, on grounds of basic consistency and justice, be taken into moral consideration.

Given what we have seen from Derrida thus far, it should be clear that he would endorse the basic position advanced by Bentham and Singer and that he would also subscribe to the surface dimensions of the logic of extending moral consideration to all sentient beings. And yet, Derrida does not pick up on these threads of Bentham's statement in his remarks (nor does he mention Singer's work, with which he is almost certainly familiar). Rather, he focuses on how Bentham's question ("The question is not, Can they *reason?* nor, Can they *talk?* but, Can they *suffer?*") has the potential for revolutionizing both the ontological and proto-ethical dimensions of the question of the animal.

With regard to the proto-ethical dimension of this question that I have been unpacking, Derrida would have us read Bentham's focus on suffering in a way that is rather different from Singer's. Rather than examining animals' capacity to feel pleasure and pain or their having preferences for certain states of affairs over others, Derrida uses Bentham's question to broach the issue of the embodied exposure of animals, their finitude and vulnerability. While the surface level of Bentham's discourse speaks in terms of capacities and faculties (*Can* they suffer?), Derrida wants to suggest that capacities are not the final foundation of animal ethics. In other words, the question of the animal as it posed here—that is, of whether an animal can suffer and how much moral weight that suffering should have—is not the primordial matter in ethical relations with animals. Rather, the question points toward and contains within itself the trace of something more basic: an interruptive encounter with animal suffering that calls for and provokes thought.

As such, the discursive *question* of the animal is already a *response* to some thing or some event that has preceded it. Whether or not such an event is explicitly remarked by Bentham or other animal ethicists, the question nevertheless testifies to the event.

If one wishes to understand what is at stake in the Derridean approach to animal ethics, one would have to pass through this idea of the event, of the pre- or proto-ethical encounter that gives rise to the question of the animal as well as the configuration and elaboration of any positive animal ethics. In figuring the question of the animal as a response to an interruptive encounter with other animals, Derrida is, of course, linking his thought with Levinas's discourse on ethics, which also takes its point of departure from an encounter with the face of the Other. But, as Derrida is well aware, Levinas more or less limits his thought of the face to the realm of the human; thus, by including other animals in his reflections on ethics, Derrida is addressing and contesting a serious limitation in Levinas's discourse, as well as those contemporary discourses that remain tributary to the anthropocentric orbit of Levinas's writings. The chief point to underscore here is that, for Derrida, what gives rise to ethical debates over animals is not simply a concern for fairness or rationality in one's moral reasoning. To be sure, these things have their place in discussions concerning norms and policy, but exclusive focus on rationality and argument in animal ethics has a tendency to make us overlook the events and encounters that give rise to our thinking on these matters. Derrida is suggesting that one is perhaps less moved, ethically and even emotively speaking, by the recognition of an animal's "ability" or "capacity" for suffering as by an encounter with an animal's *in*ability or *in*capacity to avoid pain, its fleshly vulnerability and exposure to wounding. Much as Levinas often locates the disruptive power of the face in the vulnerability and expressivity of the body, Derrida sees the embodied vulnerability of animals as the site where one's egoism is called into question and where compassion is called for:

> Being able to suffer is no longer a power, it is a possibility without power, a possibility of the impossible. Mortality resides there, as the most radical means of thinking the finitude that we share with animals, the mortality that belongs to the very finitude of life, to the experience of compassion, to the possibility of sharing the possibility

of this nonpower, the possibility of this impossibility, the anguish of this vulnerability and the vulnerability of this anguish.   (*AIA*, 396)

Thus, on Derrida's reading, Bentham's question does not send us directly or simply in the direction of argumentation and debate over the nature, extent, and moral weight of animal suffering. That has been the dominant reception of his question in the Anglo-American philosophical tradition, and it is has led to an entire field of inquiry focused on determining whether animals actually suffer and to what extent this can be confirmed empirically, and what the normative and legal implications of these empirical findings are. Given the philosophical skepticism over animal suffering in some quarters[22] and the general public ignorance concerning the conditions in which many animals live and die, these debates certainly serve an important ethical and political purpose. But they also tend to deflect the more difficult and disruptive dimensions of human-animal relations, especially the finitude and embodied exposure that human beings share with animals.[23]

If Derrida focuses nearly exclusively on this more difficult dimension, it is in order to note that the force of the encounter with the "face" of other animals is *undeniable*. And this is the case, he insists, whether we affirm or deny the animal's face, whether we respond affirmatively to the encounter or disavow it. Both responses—negation and affirmation—testify to the encounter's force and to the fact that the vulnerability and expressivity of the face pierce and affect us. It is this structure of affect that cannot be denied and that philosophy has had such difficulty incorporating. Modern philosophy, true to its Cartesian and scientific aspirations, is interested in the indubitable rather than the undeniable. Philosophers want proof that animals actually suffer, that animals are aware of their suffering, and they require an argument for why animal suffering should count on an equal par with human suffering. But the conditions of possibility for this debate are the coexposure and shared finitude of human beings and animals and the simple fact that animal suffering has the capacity to disrupt and affect human beings—not universally and not always to the same extent, to be sure, but commonly and frequently enough to give rise to the "war" over compassion toward animals. Derrida's thinking here seems to be that working through the question of the animal at this level, at the level of proto-ethical exposure, will challenge the metaphysical grounding of modern ethics and politics and reorient thought along alternative lines. It is in this sense that he argues that Bentham's question has the potential to change the nature of the philosophical question of the animal:

> No one can deny the suffering, fear or panic, the terror or fright that humans witness in certain animals. . . . The response to the question "can they suffer?" leaves no doubt. In fact it has never left any room for doubt; it precedes the indubitable, is older than it. No doubt either, then, for the possibility of our giving vent to a surge of compassion, even if it is then misunderstood, repressed, or denied, held in respect. Before the *undeniable* of this response (yes, they suffer, like us who suffer for them and with them), before this response that precedes all other questions, the problematic changes ground and base.
>
> (AIA, 396–7)

What would be the consequences for animal ethics and politics if we began from and passed through this thought? This is a question to which I shall return in the final section of this chapter.

At the proto-ethical level, then, Derrida has insisted that there is a certain disruptive force in animal suffering, one that affects and challenges us prior to any reflection or debates we might have on the ethical status of animals. One of the more provocative aspects of Derrida's approach to the question of the animal, and one that further distinguishes his thought from Levinas's, is that he does not limit the interruptive capacity of the animal simply to its vulnerability and susceptibility to wounding and suffering. While vulnerability is no doubt an exemplary "site" of interruption, one should not mistake this exemplary mode of exposure for the totality of modes of proto-ethical encounters (this is a point I also stressed in the previous chapter on Levinas). There are various ways in which animals might interrupt us, challenge our standard ways of thinking, and call us to responsibility—and many of these ways could be located more or less within the sphere of the proto-ethical.

In what is perhaps the most remarkable moment of all his texts on the question of the animal, Derrida relates one of these nonstandard, proto-ethical encounters with an animal, specifically with a cat, in his essay "The Animal That Therefore I Am." It will be useful for my purpose here of trying to understand Derrida's thought on the question of the animal to digress from the general account and examine this particular moment in his text with some care. My aim here will be to gain a better understanding of the proto-ethical dimensions of his thought but also to understand how this dimension gives rise to Derrida's extended confrontation with the anthropocentrism of ontotheological humanism.

AFTER ALL THIS TIME . . .

In framing his discussion of this peculiar encounter with a cat, Derrida asks: *"Depuis le temps, peut-on dire que l'animal nous regarde?"* (*AIA*, 372). David Wills, the English translator of this essay, suggests in a footnote that this phrase can be translated as, "Since so long ago, can we say that the animal has been our concern?" In a sense, this is the question we have been examining from the outset: Has the question of the animal been at issue in Derrida work "*depuis le temps,*" despite the lack of attention given to it by many of his readers? I have tried to argue thus far that it is no doubt the case that Derrida has long been concerned with the status of animals, not only in the history of philosophy but in his own work as well. I have also suggested that we can take him at his word when he tells us that "the question of the living and of the living animal" has always been for him "the most important and decisive question" (*AIA*, 402). But there is another, more obvious sense that can be given to Derrida's question, which David Wills privileges in this translation of the same phrase: "Since so long ago, can we say that the animal has been looking at us?" It is perhaps this latter question that confronts Derrida when, in "The Animal That Therefore I Am," he casts a glance back at his previous writings on animals. This question is a response to a singular event,[24] the event of finding oneself under the gaze of the other animal. Perhaps all of Derrida's writings on animals bear a trace of such events.

Derrida's "example" of the event at issue here is an encounter with a cat or, to be more precise, an encounter with the gaze of a cat. And not just any cat. Derrida is quick to insist that although he often makes recourse to animal figures throughout his writings, the gaze of the cat that he is referring to in this instance is not the figure of a cat, of the kind we find, for example, in Baudelaire's or Rilke's poetry or in Buber's reflections on the cat's gaze.[25] The cat that Derrida is talking about here is "a real cat, truly, believe me, *a little cat*. . . . It doesn't silently enter the room as an allegory for all the cats on earth, the felines that traverse myths and religions, literature and fables" (*AIA*, 372). And nor is it just any gaze. The gaze that this little cat directs toward him occurs at an extremely odd moment: *when he is stark naked.* It occurs, Derrida tells us, when the cat follows him into the bathroom to eat her breakfast but immediately demands to leave the bathroom upon seeing him naked. When this happens, when he finds himself "caught naked, in silence" by the cat's gaze, Derrida says he has trouble

> repressing a reflex dictated by immodesty. Trouble keeping silent within me a protest against the indecency. Against the impropriety that comes of finding oneself naked, one's sex exposed, stark naked before a cat that looks at you without moving, just to see. . . . [Here we have] the single, incomparable and original experience of impropriety that would come from appearing in truth naked, in front of the in-sistent gaze of the animal, a benevolent or pitiless gaze, surprised or cognizant. (*AIA*, 372)

It is with this moment in mind, when he finds himself caught naked under the gaze of a cat and not easily able to overcome his feeling of em-barrassment, that Derrida asks himself the autobiographical question that will guide his reflections for "The Autobiographical Animal" con-ference where he is delivering this paper: Who am I at this moment?

> I often ask myself, just to see, *who I am*—and who I am (following) at the moment when, caught naked, in silence, by the gaze of an ani-mal, for example, the eyes of a cat, I have trouble, yes a bad time over-coming my embarrassment.
> Whence this malaise? (*AIA*, 373)

Although Derrida does not mention it, we know the Nietzschean re-sponse to this question: that we are ashamed of being seen naked not because the "wild animal" inside us is exposed in such moments but rather because a "naked human being is generally a shameful sight" and the modern European human being in particular is a "tame" and "sick, sickly crippled animal . . . almost an abortion, scarce half made up, weak, awkward." Consequently, we good Europeans can scarcely dispense with either clothing or morality for covering up this shameful animal and making it appear respectable.[26] I doubt very much that Derrida would contest Nietzsche's claims here, and he as much as confirms them when, reflecting on his shame, he writes: "Ashamed of what and before whom? Ashamed of being naked as an animal" (AIA, 373). The shame that Derrida feels when caught naked by the gaze of his cat—and I suspect he is not alone in this feeling—is the shame that comes from being completely exposed and unclothed, just like an animal, in the face of the other's gaze. Naked as a jaybird, if you will.

And yet this quasi-Nietzschean response raises its own questions. What does it mean to say that one is "naked as an animal"? Can we say, in all rigor, that an animal *is* naked, that is, that an animal exists in nudity? And *if* we assume that animals are themselves without knowledge of being naked (Derrida will not go so far as to make this assumption), why would being caught naked under their gaze give rise to a feeling of shame on our part? As Derrida notes, it is generally believed that only human beings are capable of being or existing as naked because only we know what nudity is *as such*. Clothing oneself would thereby figure in the list of man's essential "propers" or properties, those unique qualities and characteristics that distinguish human beings from animals. Only human beings clothe themselves, common wisdom tells us, because only human beings are capable of feeling shame regarding their naked bodies. This trait along with other supposedly unique human characteristics, such as reason, speech, a relation to death, ethics, ek-sistence, and so on, form a configuration that clearly and decisively delimits the human being from the animal that increasingly encroaches on our human uniqueness.

From the perspective of common sense, and good philosophical sense as well, Derrida's feeling of shame in being caught naked would only serve to confirm his human uniqueness. The fact that he feels this shame when under the gaze of *an animal* is rather odd but can perhaps be explained away as a category mistake, a naïve and misplaced anthropomorphism. As the reader might suspect, however, things are not that simple. Derrida is not certain of who he is in this instance—is his shame human or animal? Is he "ashamed *like* an animal that no longer has the sense of nudity? Or on the contrary, *like* a man who retains the sense of nudity? Who am I therefore? Who is it that I am (following)? Whom should this be asked of if not the other? And perhaps of the cat itself?"

(*AIA*, 374). To be certain of what is taking place in this particular instance requires placing one's trust in a set of categories and concepts (self, other, human, animal) that are being called into question by the encounter. What Derrida is describing is not an encounter with the gaze of "an animal" (in general), but finding oneself *being seen* by the uncanny gaze of a particular animal, a cat, this little female cat that, even though it is domesticated and all too familiar, nonetheless retains the capacity for challenging that familiarity.[27]

In truth, however, Derrida is struck by the cat's gaze prior to even these minimal conceptualizations (cat, little, female). Thus, when he says that the cat he is referring to is not a cat "figure" but is in fact a "real cat, truly, believe me, *a little cat*," he is aware of the inadequacy of such language and the problematic nature of the distinction between such concepts as "figure" and "real." What Derrida is trying to gesture toward, however awkwardly, is something for which existing modes of language are not particularly well equipped: the thought of this particular "cat" as an absolutely unique and irreplaceable entity, one whose uncanny gaze cannot find its substitute in the gaze of another animal.

> If I say "it is a real cat" that sees me naked, it is in order to mark its
> unsubstitutable [*irremplaçable*] singularity. . . . It is true that I identify
> it as a male or female cat. But even before that identification, I see
> it as *this* irreplaceable living being that one day enters my space, enters this place where it can encounter me, see me, even see me naked.
> Nothing can ever take away from me the certainty that what we have
> here is an existence that refuses to be conceptualized [*rebelle à tout
> concept*].   (*AIA*, 378–79)

This has been one of Derrida's central questions since his earliest work, namely, how to refer *in* language and concepts to that which precisely resists conceptualization. In commenting on this passage, postmodern theorist Steve Baker thus misses the point when he suggests that the "sophisticated deconstructive moves" we have come to associate with Derrida's work have here been abandoned when he tries to make reference to a "real" animal. Baker says he finds it "both instructive and extremely funny to observe Derrida's desperation" in trying to assure his readers that the cat he is referring to is to be understood, without irony, as a "real" cat.[28] Baker's response to this passage betrays a typical misunderstanding of "deconstruction" as a project that seeks to suspend reference altogether, abandoning us within the prison-house of language. Rather than suspending the possibility of reference, Derrida has throughout his work instead sought to *complicate* traditional theories of reference.[29] At stake here, among other things, are a number of questions that concern not only the problems of employing reductive language to refer to the Other, but also finding a nonreductive way to mark the effects of the Other within the very discourses (for example, philosophy) that are grounded on a forgetting of the alterity of the other.

In insisting on the unsubstitutable singularity of the cat, then, Derrida is contesting the possibility of fully reducing this particular cat to an object of knowledge, whether philosophical or otherwise. Derrida *does not know* who this cat is at the moment of the gaze any more than he knows who he is. His encounter with the cat takes place in a *contretemps*, in a time out of joint, prior to and outside of knowledge and identification. The scene of nonknowing in which one finds oneself exposed to the other animal is somewhat akin to madness, which is why Derrida calls it a "deranged theatrics" (*AIA,* 380) and finds the words of the Cheshire Cat in *Alice in Wonderland* particularly fitting for describing it: "We're all mad here. I'm mad. You're mad" (*AIA,* 379). When trying to answer the autobiographical question "Who am I?" in such moments of madness, Derrida, not surprisingly, finds a properly "philosophical" response to be impossible.[30] One can only ask the question "Who am I?" once one has recovered from the madness, come back to oneself, and regained intellectual composure. *Who I am at the moment of madness* is impossible to determine, for the "I"—whether it is conceived in terms of the subject, cogito, transcendental unity of apperception, transcendental ego, or self-consciousness—is not fully there to synthesize and make sense of the experience. The I, strictly speaking, emerges only *after* such "mad" moments of exposure to the other animal. The question "Who am I?" thus seems, for Derrida to necessitate a rather paradoxical answer: "'I am inasmuch as I am *after* the animal' or 'I am inasmuch as I am *alongside* the animal'" (*AIA,* 379).

In terms of the proto-ethical dimensions of this encounter, then, we can say that according to Derrida's account I come to myself and arrive at self-consciousness only in and through other animals, that is, other living beings, whether human, animal, or otherwise. Such encounters do not obey the laws of the Hegelian dialectic of recognition; rather, they occur in a time and space that precedes and gives rise to the possibility of any recognition. Such encounters are specifically proto-ethical in that I affirm, or say "yes," to the Other before I can negate or disavow the Other's impact. The Other leaves a trace of the shock of encounter within me, and how I respond to that trace—whether I affirm or negate, avow or disavow—constitutes ethics, properly speaking. The main stakes of Derrida's work on the question of the animal is to insist that ethical thought in relation to animals begins in and attests to such proto-ethical encounters—which is to say, animal ethics is not simply a matter of theoretical consistency and rationality.

Animal Subjects

At this point, we are in a better position to examine the ontological dimensions of Derrida's thought, which, as I previously mentioned, are among the most difficult aspects of his work on the question of the animal. The focus I have just given to the autobiographical component of the question of the animal serves as a useful avenue for accessing the salient ontological issues inasmuch as the questions concerning subjectivity and madness I have examined help to point out the limitations of the ontology underlying traditional conceptions of animal ethics and politics. In his autobiographical account of the encounter with his cat, Derrida is intent upon underscoring the "event"-like nature of the encounter and the way in which its force jumbles his experience of time, self, and being. This kind of encounter with the alterity of another animal helps to expose the limitations and shortcomings of our existing philosophical language about animals as well as corresponding ethical and political theories, whether pro- or anti-animal.

If dominant forms of ethical theory—from Kantianism to care ethics to moral rights theory—are unwilling to make a place for animals within their scope of consideration, it is clear that emerging theories of ethics that are more open and expansive with regard to animals are able to develop their positions only by making other, equally serious kinds of exclusions concerning animals. First, in order to communicate with dominant theories of ethics, pro-animal positions are obliged to structure their ethical reasoning in line with the guiding assumptions and categories of ethical theory, such as moral agency and patiency, universalizability, self and other, reciprocity, and so forth. Most of these categories originate in discourses that are fundamentally anthropocentric, and it is only through considerable effort that they can be bent into the service of animals. Second, pro-animal theorists are further obliged to present us with an idea of other animals that views them in philosophically acceptable terms, which in today's philosophical climate amounts to "scientific" and "biological" terms. Animals are not viewed as fundamentally alien to human language and concepts but rather as coextensive with the scientific discourses that purport to describe them. Consequently, animal ethicists rarely make recourse to poetic, literary, or artistic descriptions of animals—descriptions that might help us to see animals otherwise, which is to say, otherwise than the perspectives offered by the biological sciences, common sense, or the anthropocentric "wisdom" of the ages.

What these two limitations amount to, in short, are a set of quasi-invisible constraints that guide animal ethics and politics in a seemingly predestined direction. The overarching aim of pro-animal theorists seems to be, first, to demonstrate that one or another longstanding ethical theory should (logically, definitionally, or conceptually) include animals within its scope and, second, to use this ethical framework to ground arguments for full standing for animals within the legal and political sphere. This strategy makes use of what Peter Singer calls a "logic of liberation," a kind of moral and political reasoning that extends and expands liberatory discourses by way of analogical argumentation. This is such a common way of thinking about animal ethics and other progressive political movements that very few theorists or activists would bother to question its underlying premises. But Derrida's work on animals is intended to pose a series of questions at this exact level. What is at stake in this kind of thinking and strategy? How does it both open and foreclose certain ethical and political possibilities? How might it unwittingly create new forms of exclusion and hierarchies? Does it do justice to animals? Does it do justice to humans? Moreover, can we and should we rely on either common sense or scientific accounts of what it means to be "human" or "animal"? Are either of these terms adequate for ethico-political thought and practice?

Derrida speaks explicitly to the promise and peril of thinking about animals within existing ethical, political, and legal frameworks in his interview with Elizabeth Roudinesco. Here he argues that invoking humanist and anthropocentric legal and moral frameworks in the service of animal rights is a "disastrous contradiction" (VA, 65), especially when this strategy is understood in relation to the liberatory and radically egalitarian impulses of these movements. There is a peculiar irony at work when animal rights theorists and animal liberationists employ classical humanist and anthropocentric criteria to argue for granting animals certain rights or protecting them from suffering, for *it is these very criteria that have served historically to justify violence toward animals*. It might seem that animal ethicists would, as radical environmentalists have done, take as their main aim a critical analysis of the exclusionary and hierarchical tendencies of classical moral theory with an eye toward developing an altogether or substantially different conception of ethics. Surely, the exclusionary and hierarchical nature of traditional moral theory and practice should be held in deep suspicion by those who argue on behalf of the excluded and degraded. However, precisely the opposite has been the case with the vast majority of animal theory and activism. The same kinds of line drawing, exclusions, and value rankings we find in humanist ethical theory are widespread throughout pro-animal discourses. Rather than rejecting hierarchical schemas in the name of a different kind of ethics, most animal ethicists believe that the hierarchies have simply been inappropriately or unfairly drawn. The inclusion of animals (and, we should note that not *all* animals are included by the dominant approaches to animal ethics) within our moral calculus is, for many of these theorists at least, a matter of getting things "right," of drawing moral boundaries in a rationally satisfying and rigorous manner. As I argued in my discussion of Levinas, this debate over line drawing and moral considerability has been the main point of contention and site of theorizing among animal ethicists, and I further argued in that chapter that this entire approach to animal ethics is a mistake, perhaps the most serious mistake that has occurred in the field. There is no a priori reason to grant that ethics must develop along humanist and anthropocentric lines, or that we should stretch and expand humanist liberatory discourses to include previously excluded groups such as animals. Rather than taking this approach for granted and as somehow the only rational and logical manner of proceeding in philosophical debates over the ethical status of animals, we should see it instead for what it is: a more or less useful strategy with both beneficial and pernicious consequences.

I have already explained how Derrida lends his support and sympathy to the beneficial and progressive aspects of pro-animal theories and practices. While this dimension of his thought is important to underscore, both for situating Derrida in the wider context of Continental philosophical thought (which is predominantly silent or negative about animals and ethics) and in order to underscore the affirmative and ethical impetus of his work, there is—at least in my estimation—nothing particularly novel about his explicit political positions on issues involving animals or the manner in which they are articulated. In fact, as I noted, many readers familiar with Anglo-American philosophical debates on the issues will likely be frustrated with his unwillingness to speak and write more programmatically about these issues and to elaborate his positions in more detail.

Where Derrida's thought *does* become rather novel and provocative with regard to the question of the animal concerns his reflections on the pernicious consequences of standard philosophical approaches to animal ethics and the manner in which we might begin to circumvent them. At this level, Derrida offers an important diagnosis of what I just referred to as the "quasi-invisible constraints" that guide progressive thought about animals and that rebind these potentially liberatory discourses to the metaphysical tradition they seek to displace. The guiding thread for this critical analysis concerns the critique of the "metaphysics of subjectivity" that Derrida associates with Heidegger and other antihumanist theorists. In line with these theorists, many of Derrida's earliest texts were dedicated to uncovering the remnants of a metaphysics of subjectivity in contemporary philosophy in the form of a metaphysics of "presence," where presence is understood in terms of self-presence (lucid and transparent self-consciousness) and presence to the other (an other that is ultimately seen as reducible to the same/self). The aim of these works is, in the most general sense, to demonstrate that the discourses that have pretensions to full presence cannot be rigorously maintained and that various forms of "static" (interruption, *différance,* supplementarity, and so forth) are invariably at work wherever full presence is sought. The central example of a notion of the self based on full presence is the "human" subject in modern philosophical discourse. The human is distinguished from its others (animal, nature, childhood, infancy, madness, and so on) inasmuch as the human, through consciousness and self-awareness, is deemed to have more or less direct and transparent access to itself and the other and is able to maintain self-identity in encounters with the other. In the Western philosophical tradition, this notion of the human has served especially frequently as a means of distinguishing humans from nonhuman animals, which, it is argued, lack consciousness, self-awareness, language, and other capacities that would allow for presence.

Rather than displacing this anthropocentric metaphysics of subjectivity and presence, many animal rights theorists have tried to assimilate animals to the traditional model of the human. It is often argued that animals do, in fact, have the capacities traditionally denied to them (self-awareness, consciousness) and that animals are, in fact, full subjects. Tom Regan, for instance, has argued that animals are worthy of moral respect inasmuch as they, like human beings, are "subjects of a life." He writes that each of us, whether a human or animal individual, is an

> experiencing subject of a life, a conscious creature having an individual welfare that has importance to us whatever our usefulness to others. We want and prefer things, believe and feel things, recall and expect things. And all these dimensions of our life, including our pleasure and pain, our enjoyment and suffering, our satisfaction and frustration, our continued existence or our untimely death—all make a difference to the quality of our life as lived, as experienced, by us as individuals.[31]

Regan's statement is no doubt true about certain animals, especially animals with "higher-order" cognitive capacities. But the paradox of this premise about the shared subjectivity of humans and animals is that it excludes most animals from its scope—a point that is not lost on Regan. He notes that his theory of animal rights strictly applies only to mammals one year of age and older.[32] Although Regan has no desire to use his theory to create a new set of exclusions that will place those animals not having these traits outside the scope of moral concern (he argues instead for a charitable approach to line drawing), this is precisely its effect. For it is clear that many animals will never meet these criteria and will never demonstrate this particular kind of subjective life—and the same is true for many human beings. And, if we grant privileged moral status to those beings with a certain kind of subjective life, then the logical consequences within this moral framework are clear: those beings lacking subjectivity have a lower or nonexistent ethical status.

This logic and the consequences (hierarchical, exclusionary, etc.) that follow from it are the kind of quasi-invisible constraints that limit and mold dominant discourses on animal ethics and against which Derrida seeks to develop an alternative idea of human-animal ethical relations. And it is precisely in view of the social, political, and philosophical implications of these discourses that he is critical of the juridicism and legal reformism of the animal rights movement. In my reading of Agamben, I showed that Derrida has little or no faith in the idea that existing legal institutions can be reformed in order to accommodate animals.[33] Based as they are on a metaphysics of subjectivity and presence, it is clear that modern legal institutions will simply never regard animals as full legal subjects anymore than anthropocentric moral discourse will ever regard animals as full ethical subjects. And this should come as no surprise, given that traditional legal and moral discourse emerges out of an anthropocentric and metaphysical horizon that is grounded on human chauvinism and exceptionalism. The dominant strategy of trying to reform this tradition rather than calling it radically into question is understandable but should be seen ultimately as a failure of imagination on the part of animal rights theorists.

Derrida would have us recast the question of the animal along entirely different lines and try to imagine other ways of conceiving of animal life and ethical relations between human beings and animals. The first thing to which Derrida would have us attend is the manner in which the concept of subjectivity has been constituted historically. Thus far I have focused on the anthropocentric aspects of the metaphysics of subjectivity, but Derrida argues that the meaning of subjectivity is constituted through a network of exclusionary relations that goes well beyond a generic human-animal distinction. He has coined the term "carnophallogocentrism" to refer to this network of relations and in order to highlight the *sacrificial* (carno), *masculine* (phallo), and *speaking* (logo) dimensions of classical conceptions of subjectivity. What Derrida is trying to get at with this concept is how the metaphysics of subjectivity works to exclude not just animals from the status of being full subjects but other beings as well, in particular women, children, various minority groups, and other Others who are taken to be lacking in one or another of the basic traits of subjectivity. Just as many animals have and continue to be excluded from basic legal protections, so, as Derrida notes, there have been "many 'subjects' among mankind who are not recognized as subjects"[34] and who receive the same kind of violence typically directed at animals. This would position certain groups of human beings in a similar space of marginalization alongside animals; furthermore, this shared position suggests that thinking through the processes of human and animal marginalization together can be useful for uncovering the functioning and consequences of the metaphysics of subjectivity. No doubt the marginalization of different groups of human beings, on the one hand, and animals, on the other hand, has occurred along distinct historical and institutional lines, and the effects of this marginalization have been uneven. But joint examination of human and animal subjection can help to render undeniably clear the potentially violent nature of the exclusionary logic of the metaphysics of subjectivity. Ecofeminists such as Carol Adams[35] and sociologists such as David Nibert[36] have made parallel arguments in other contexts to this same effect. And the ultimate point that these authors seek to make is that bringing animals within the scope of existing forms of moral and legal subjectivity is not a genuine solution to the problems under discussion here. And the reason for this should already be clear: these inclusions come at the price of a different set of exclusions, in which other animals and other groups of human beings are deemed "nonsubjects" and potentially unworthy of legal and moral consideration. What needs to be reformed, or rather transformed, is the juridicism and exclusionary logic that underlies our dominant practices and ways of thinking and the legal and political institutions that encode and reinforce these practices.

But the neologism "carno-phallogocentrism" is intended to do more than indicate the multiple axes of exclusions that have functioned historically in the development of the metaphysics of subjectivity. Derrida is also arguing at the same time that being a carnivore is at the very heart of becoming a full subject in contemporary society. Participating, whether directly or indirectly, in the processes and rituals of killing and eating animal flesh is almost a necessary prerequisite of being a subject. Those individuals who, through eating a vegan or vegetarian diet and trafficking in animal rights politics, seek to resist carnivorous practices and institutions are often viewed as being outside the dominant forms of being a subject. In Derrida's words, "carnivorous sacrifice is essential to the structure of subjectivity, which is also to say to the founding of the intentional subject."[37] The subject, typically male, "accepts sacrifice and eats flesh."[38] As evidence for this claim, Derrida poses the following question concerning a prototypical subject, in this case a head of State: "Who would stand any chance of becoming a *chef d'Etat* (a head of

State), and of thereby acceding "to the head," by publicly, and therefore exemplarily, declaring him- or herself to be a vegetarian? The *chef* must be an eater of flesh."[39] Once again, the point here is that becoming a subject is not a morally and legally neutral process but is structured by a number of symbolic and literal constraints that are potentially violent and exclusionary toward all beings deemed to be nonsubjects, especially animals. As such, Derrida's deconstructionist approach to a critique of subjectivity works toward "a reinterpretation of the whole apparatus of boundaries"[40] that is aimed less at expanding the boundaries and more at reworking them so as to overcome them and think through and beyond them.

Given that a politically progressive vegetarianism is perhaps the most direct challenge to carno-phallogocentrism, it might seem that this practice is the ethicopolitical telos of Derrida's thought on the question of the animal. As we have seen, Derrida himself criticizes standard arguments against vegetarianism and appears to align himself with those discourses and practices that aim at maximum respect toward animals. And Derrida scholar David Wood has made an argument that explicitly links deconstruction and vegetarianism as a means of resisting the effects of carno-phallogocentrism. Wood argues that:

> Carnophallogocentrism is not a dispensation of Being toward which resistance is futile; it is a mutually reinforcing network of powers, schemata of domination, and investments that has to reproduce itself to stay in existence. Vegetarianism is not just about substituting beans for beef; it is—at least potentially—a site of proliferating resistance to that reproduction. If we allow the imminences and pressures (and ghosts and cries and suffering) to which I have been yielding to have their say [Wood is referring to a number of issues he has raised earlier in his essay—the breaching of the human-animal boundary, the reduction of biological diversity, and the massive slaughtering of animals], we might well end up insisting that "deconstruction is vegetarianism."[41]

Here Wood is making the kind of linkage between vegetarianism and deconstruction that Derrida has ventured between justice and deconstruction in "Force of Law." For Derrida, deconstruction (*if* it exists, as he always adds) is justice, understood as a passion for the impossible and a relation with an alterity that remains irreducibly Other. On this line of thought, even though discourses *about* the Other (moral, legal, political, etc.) will always remain deconstructible, the passion *for* the Other is not. This passion is the animating force of deconstruction, and without it deconstruction would never get underway. For Wood, vegetarianism is a similar kind of deconstructive passion, one that contests reductive discourses and practices toward animals and aims to respect the alterity of animals. Inasmuch as these passions are the animating drive behind vegetarianism, Wood is no doubt correct to align deconstruction and vegetarianism. But this alignment also has the effect of protecting vegetarianism from a deconstructive critique, if, that is, we consider vegetarianism to be (like justice) un-deconstructible. Wood himself does not offer much in the way of a deconstruction of vegetarianism, and in this he mirrors much of "progressive" discourse on "ethical vegetarianism." It is often assumed by ethical vegetarians that vegetarianism is a kind of ultimate moral ideal, one that exempts its practitioners from any kind of violence toward animals and that substantially challenges the existing anthropocentric ethicopolitical order.

While I would certainly not want to disparage the efforts of vegetarians to limit violence toward animals in their personal lives and in public institutions and practices involving the slaughter and consumption of animals, I think it is important also to underscore that vegetarianism is itself fundamentally deconstructible. Vegetarianism is not just a passion for other animals but a series of practices involving animals and a series of discourses about animals. And if we follow the logic of Derrida's thought on the question of the animal, then it is necessary both to support vegetarianism's progressive potential but also interrogate its limitations. I have already shown how animal ethics in general (and animal rights theory, in particular) tends to reinforce the very metaphysics of subjectivity it seeks to undercut inasmuch as animal ethicists rely on a shared subjectivity among human beings and animals to ground their theories. But there are other limitations in vegetarian and pro-animal practices that should be noted. First, no matter how rigorous one's vegetarianism might be, there is simply no way to nourish oneself in advanced, industrial countries that does not involve harm to animal life (and human life, as well) in direct and indirect forms. (And I should note that it is rather curious that Wood focuses on vegetarianism rather than veganism in his essay, inasmuch as the latter diet is, when approached ethically, far more rigorous, as it is premised on eliminating as much as is possible the massive mistreatment animals undergo not only in the meat industry but also in the dairy and animal-byproducts industries as well.) Simply tracking the processes by which one's food gets to the table is enough to disabuse any consumer of the notion that a vegetarian diet is "cruelty free." As such, a vegetarian diet within the context of advanced, industrial societies is, at best, a significant challenge to dominant attitudes and practices toward animals, but it remains far from the kind of ethical ideal it is sometimes purported to be. Second, there are other ethical stakes involved in eating that go beyond the effects consumption of meat and animal byproducts has on animals. All diets, even organic and vegetarian diets, have considerable negative effects on the natural environment and the human beings who produce and harvest food. Consequently, if we consider ethical vegetarianism to constitute an ethical stopping point, these other concerns will be overlooked. And it is precisely these other concerns, concerns about other, often-overlooked forms of violence, that should *also* impassion a deconstructive approach to the question of the animal.

Although these critical points are certainly in line with the logic of a deconstructive approach to animal ethics, they do not form the focus of Derrida's analysis. Derrida draws attention, instead, to a different limitation inherent to pro-animal ethics and politics, one that he associates with "interventionist violence" (*AIA,* 394) against animals. The violence at issue here takes a *symbolic* rather than literal form, and this symbolic violence against animals, Derrida seems to think, is one of the most pressing philosophical and metaphysical issues facing thought today. In view of this notion of symbolic violence, he makes the following statement: "Vegetarians, too, partake of animals, even of men. They practice a different mode of denegation."[42] What does he mean by this? Clearly, ethical vegetarianism aims at avoiding consumption of animal flesh—and presumably human flesh, as well. So, in what manner do vegetarians partake of animals and other beings toward which they aim to be nonviolent? Derrida's remark here is part of a complicated argument about the ethical questions concerning eating, incorporation, and violence toward the Other. While Derrida, like Levinas, posits a nonviolent opening to the Other (for Levinas, this occurs at the level of the saying, whereas in Derrida it is associated with his affirmative infrastructures, such as *Come, yes,* and *pledge*), he does not believe that a wholly nonviolent relation with the Other is possible. On his line of thought, violence is irreducible in our relations with the Other, if by nonviolence we mean a thought and practice relating to the Other that respects fully the alterity of the Other. In order to speak and think about or relate to the Other, the Other must—to some extent—be appropriated and violated, even if only symbolically. How does one respect the singularity of the Other without betraying that alterity? *Any* act of identification, naming, or relation is a betrayal of and a violence toward the Other. Of course, this should not be taken to mean that such violence is immoral or that all forms of violence are equivalent. Rather, the aim is to undercut completely the possibility of achieving good conscience in regard to questions of nonviolence toward the Other. The ideal of ethical purity is ruled out a priori as structurally impossible. And for Derrida, this should signal a substantial change in the ethical question of eating. To take vegetarianism as an example, the ethical question should not be "How do I achieve an ethically pure, cruelty-free diet?" but rather, "What is the best, most respectful, most grateful, and also most giving way of relating"[43] to animals and other Others. The latter approach lies at the bottom of an animal ethics that is impassioned by an ideal of maximum respect for animals and that structurally disallows complacency or good conscience of any sort.

Letting Go

I have at this point arrived at a juncture where I can turn to the heart of Derrida's thought on the question of the animal—the point where Derrida critically engages traditional anthropocentric and ontotheological discourses on animals. Before we take up this theme, though, it will be useful to cast a glance backward and examine the points made thus far. I began by suggesting that the question of the animal is by no means a minor aspect of Derrida's thought but is in fact a central question throughout his writings, from the earliest to the most recent. This point is made evident by examining the way in which many of Derrida's "infrastructures" are formulated so as to include both human and nonhuman life forms, and noticing that his early and recent texts on ethics have consistently made a place for animals. I further argued that Derrida's writings make clear that he holds a concrete ethicopolitical position that has substantial overlap with the theories and practices of contemporary animal rights and liberation and that this concrete position is in turn informed by a proto-ethical imperative that arises from a face-to-face encounter with the Other animal that radicalizes animal ethics and disrupts any possible form of good conscience in this field. It is the proto-ethical imperative that also gives rise to his thoroughgoing critique of the anthropocentric metaphysical tradition, which will be my topic for the remainder of this chapter.

My discussion of Derrida thus far has been largely expository and rather uncritical, especially in comparison with the discussions of Heidegger, Levinas, and Agamben in the foregoing chapters. The reason for this difference of approach is twofold: First, Derrida's writings on animality have been badly misread in most cases and are still in need of careful exposition.[44] Second, I am in broad agreement with Derrida's general approach and his arguments on the points examined thus far. Among contemporary Continental philosophers, Derrida is by far the most useful and insightful thinker in the domain of questions surrounding animality, and my general support of his approach reflects my respect for his original approach to the very difficult questions encountered in this domain of thought.

In the remainder of this chapter, however, the tenor of my analysis of Derrida's work will shift considerably. I will offer a charitable account of his critical engagement with the anthropocentrism of the metaphysical tradition, but in so doing I will lay out where I think his arguments go awry and where the argument developed in this book departs from his. In brief, I will argue that despite Derrida's critical engagement with metaphysical anthropocentrism, his thought does not offer a genuine challenge to this tradition and remains beholden to its logic and conceptuality.

To begin, it will be helpful to look briefly at Derrida's most sustained critical encounters with anthropocentrism in the metaphysical tradition. Although he has written at some length on Aristotle,[45] Descartes, Kant, Levinas, and Lacan[46] with an eye toward their writings on animality, he has devoted the most attention to a critical engagement with Heidegger's discourse on animals and the human-animal distinction. The specific reasons for this preponderant focus on Heidegger (as opposed to, say, Descartes) are never, to my knowledge at least, explicitly discussed by Derrida; but I think that I can make a reasonable inference to the best explanation. Heidegger is most likely Derrida's main focal point in elaborating the question of the animal not simply because Heidegger looms large in the background of his thought but because Heidegger's critical analysis of humanism is the best developed critique in the philosophical tradition—and a critique that *should* have opened on to the larger question of anthropocentrism in a more profound manner. That Heidegger's critique of humanism never led him to think more critically about anthropocentrism is one of the more important questions for contemporary discourses that take his work as their point of departure (which is to say, for much of Continental philosophy); additionally, Heidegger's resistance to displacements of anthropocentrism (in thinkers such as Nietzsche, Darwin, and Rilke and in twentieth-century *Lebensphilosophie* more generally) allow the reader to see very clearly where the dogmas of anthropocentrism function in his work (and in subsequent philosophy that has remained within the orbit of his thought). Derrida has drawn explicit attention to this dogmatism in one of his many essays on Heidegger. Concerning Heidegger's infamous remark that the "ape, for example, possesses organs for grasping, but it has no hand,"[47] Derrida suggests that this statement is Heidegger's "most significant, symptomatic, and seriously dogmatic."[48]

Now, this is no minor claim on Derrida's part, for it suggests that one of, if not *the,* most significant limit in Heidegger's thinking concerns animality. And given the critical importance of Heidegger for Derrida, it appears that Derrida takes Heidegger's dogmatic anthropocentrism to be one of the chief obstacles and questions for thought today. Derrida's critical readings of Heidegger on animality began most famously with his series of "Geschlecht" articles, where he problematized Heidegger's reductive analysis of animals. This analysis was continued in *Of Spirit* through an interrogation of Heidegger's denial of "world" to animals in his lecture course of 1929 and 1930, *Fundamental Concepts of Metaphysics,* to which I have already devoted considerable attention in the chapter on Heidegger. A few years later, in "'Eating Well'" Derrida extended this critical analysis of Heidegger in reference to the themes of animal killing, friendship, and subjectivity, and he also sought to link Heidegger's thought with Levinas's and other anthropocentric and humanist discourses about animals. Similarly, in *Aporias,* Derrida takes Heidegger to task for his rather questionable distinction between the "dying" proper to Dasein and the "perishing" that belongs to animals and other living beings. Derrida's general strategy in each of these critical confrontations with Heidegger is to complicate the kinds of reductive binary oppositions found in Heidegger's texts and to insist that binary oppositions fail to do justice to the multiplicity and complexity of life forms called "animal."

When questioned about his strategy of complicating binary oppositions and whether this complication is meant to erase oppositions and form an undifferentiated, homogenous group comprising human-animals, Derrida insists that he is not at all interested in blurring differences but is instead trying to re-mark differences that have been reduced, denied, or overlooked. He explains that

> if you draw a single or two single lines [between animals and human beings], then you have homogenous sets of undifferentiated societies, or groups, or structures. No, no I am not advocating the blurring of differences. On the contrary, I am trying to explain how drawing an oppositional limit itself blurs the differences, the differance and the differences, not only between man and animal, but among animal societies—there are an infinite number of animal societies, and, within the animal societies and within human society itself, so many differences.[49]

This statement nicely encapsulates the underlying logic of all of Derrida's interventions and writings on the question of the animal. He is concerned throughout all of his texts on this issue to disrupt metaphysical discourses about animals that treat each singular animal as an instance of "The Animal," a homogeneous, essentialist, and reductive category that presumes that there is something in common shared by (or lacking in) all beings labeled "animal." As I have shown in my readings of Heidegger, Levinas, and Agamben, the philosophical tradition has been particularly egregious in this respect and has only rarely accorded or given attention to the singularity of animal life. Inasmuch as Derrida seeks to contest this kind of simplistic thinking about animals, I think his work is to be applauded—for the kind of reductionism he criticizes remains rampant both in Continental and analytic philosophical circles and in dominant discourses and institutions. In order to disrupt and displace this kind of thinking, interventions of several sorts are needed—and a Derridean approach could, I believe, play an important role.

But the question that needs to be addressed is: What, precisely, is

Derrida recommending *in place* of these reductive binaries? Is he simply criticizing the philosophical tradition, or he is also offering another way of thinking about animals that would overcome, or at least proceed with an eye toward the limitations of, dominant metaphysical thinking about animals? In short, I want to ask (to paraphrase Nietzsche): Are new idols being erected here, or is it simply that old ones are being demolished?

It is clear from his published and unpublished work on this issue that Derrida is very much concerned with developing the rudiments of an alternative thought of animals. The best place to find his considered views on this issue are, once again, the essay "The Animal That Therefore I Am." Here he presents his position in terms of a reflection on "limitrophy," on what is situated at the intersection of a border, of "what abuts onto limits but also what feeds, is fed, is cared for, raised, and trained, what is cultivated on the edges of a limit" (*AIA,* 397). In order to develop an alternative thought of animal life, it would first be necessary to attend to the limitrophe nature of the border drawn between human and animal. How is this border created, nourished, maintained, and sustained? What are the linguistic and institutional forces at work around and along this border? Derrida's interventions in the history of metaphysical discourses on animals are aimed at uncovering some of these mechanisms and highlighting the dominant and hegemonic dogmas in this field of thought. But even on the most generous reading, it is clear that Derrida's work has only scratched the surface of this project of deconstructing the history of the limitrophe discourse of the human-animal distinction. Along philosophical lines, Elisabeth de Fontenay's massive volume, *Le silence des bêtes,* is something much closer to the kind of philosophical analysis needed to trace the anthropocentric underpinnings of Western metaphysical philosophy.[50] And yet, even de Fontenay's work is far from exhausting the critical historical project here, inasmuch as the functioning and sustaining of the human-animal border has a complicated history and present and requires a multidisciplinary critical approach. And it is here that one of the central axes of the emerging fields of animal studies might profitably be situated. Animal studies could take as one of its primary aims a historical and genealogical analysis of the constitution of the human-animal distinction and how this distinction has functioned across a number of institutions, practices, and discourses. Not only would this project further desediment and denaturalize the human-animal distinction, but it would also help to uncover alternative ways of conceiving of human beings and animals that have been ignored, covered over, and distorted by dominant discourses. Although Derrida was himself unable to carry through on this project, it is clear that he saw it as the gateway to any kind of alternative manner of thinking about animal life, and it further demonstrates his strategic allegiance with a certain genealogical mode of philosophizing and his indebtedness to philosophers such as Nietzsche and Foucault.

Beyond the historico-genealogical dimensions of the project of thinking otherwise about animals lies the necessity of developing an alternative ontology of animal life, an ontology in which the human-animal distinction is called radically into question. Although an evasion of ontological questions is one of the standard gestures of much of recent postmodern and poststructuralist discourse, I think it is a mistake to read Derrida's discourse as belonging to this trend. In his reflections on the question of the animal in particular, he is at pains to articulate an alternative ontological thought and concept of "animal life," one that draws thought away from the reductive accounts of animality in the history of metaphysics and closer to contemporary animal philosophers such as Deleuze and Donna Haraway. For Derrida, the chief limit of the metaphysical tradition is that it has consistently tried to reduce and even efface the differences among various forms of animal life. Any ontology that challenges this tradition will need to be antireductive and antianthropocentric to the extreme. In view of this issue, Derrida suggests that on the other side of the human, we do not find a group of beings that share a common "animality" but a heterogeneous series of beings and relationships. Thus, rather than

"the Animal" or "Animal Life," there is already a heterogeneous multiplicity of the living, or more precisely (since to say "the living" is already to say too much or not enough) a multiplicity of organizations of relations between living and dead, relations of organization or lack of organization among realms that are more and more difficult to dissociate by means of the figures of the organic and inorganic, of life and/or death. These relations are at once close and abyssal, and they can never be totally objectified. (*AIA*, 399)

This passage is extremely helpful for understanding the ontology that underlies not only Derrida's writings on the question of the animal but all of his writings on the question of life and life/death, as well as the various infrastructures he develops in his texts from the 1960s and 1970s. What we find here is a relational and machinic ontology of singularities, one that is informed as much by Nietzschean and Deleuzean materialism as by Heideggerian and Levinasian phenomenology. This is perhaps the most radical strain of Derrida's thought on the question of the animal, and it is the closest to the argument developed in this book—for this line of thought takes away the ground for making any kind of binary human-animal distinction. If what we call "animal life" is constituted by a "heterogeneous multiplicity" of entities and a "multiplicity of organizations of relations" between organic and inorganic life forms, then what sense can be made of an insuperable division between human and animal? Do not "human beings" belong to this multiplicity of beings and relations? Are we to believe that human beings are somehow exempt from the play of differences and forces, of becomings and relations? Are not "human beings" sliding constantly along a series of differences, including those that are thought to separate human from animal, animal from plant, and life in general from death? In brief, then, it is clear that the ontology Derrida offers here would forbid the possibility of making any kind of clean distinction between human and animal, not only because of the irreducible plurality of beings but also because of the multiplicity of becomings and relational structures between human and animal.

But do Derrida's ontological reflections lead him to abandon the human-animal distinction altogether? We have already seen Agamben's argument for the abandonment of this distinction in view of its role in the functioning of the anthropological machine. Agamben's argument is essentially political and, in the last analysis, anthropocentric, although I have tried to suggest that his arguments can be read and applied toward nonanthropocentric ends. It would seem, based on what we have seen thus far, that Derrida's work might add a kind of nonanthropocentric corrective and ethico-ontological supplement to Agamben's political arguments. On the ethical level, Derrida would have us understand the proto-ethical relations between human beings and animals in terms of a disruptive, face-to-face encounter between singular beings. As such, any homogenizing of human beings or animals would betray the singularity of the ethical relation as well as the beings who are themselves in relation. Whether such betrayals are *politically and strategically* necessary is a question I have examined in my reading of Levinas. But with regard to Derrida, we can see that the singularity and singular relations characteristic of human-animal ethical encounters should trouble our standard ethical concepts and any human-animal distinction that might inform ethical thought. On the ontological level, Derrida argues for a relational and machinic ontology that attends to the multiplicity of forms of animal (and human) life and the relational structures in, among, and between the various forms of animal (and human) life. To my mind, the chief conclusion to be drawn from Derrida's analysis is that the human-animal distinction is, strictly speaking, *nonsensical.* How could a simple (or even a highly refined) binary distinction approach doing justice to the complex ethical and ontological matters at stake here? I am not suggesting, of course, that there *is* a language or set of concepts that could accurately capture the ontological and ethical vision that Derrida is proposing (and it is not all clear to me that "capturing" and referencing reality are the ultimate tasks here). There can be no doubt, as Georges Bataille notes, that the world is always richer than language[51] and that language will always fail to do justice to the world. But there are failures and there are failures. The human-animal distinction is so clumsy and awkward, so lacking in rigor that one wonders what possible use it would have for *philosophers,* who so often pride themselves on the rigor of their concepts. Surely Derrida's thought, inasmuch as it is *philosophical* and follows through on the implications of his ethical and ontological analyses, would bring us to the conclusion that the human-animal distinction should be abolished or, at the very least, be treated with considerable caution and suspicion.

In his debate with John Searle, Derrida makes these very same points concerning the issue of making rigorous distinctions. When Searle accuses Derrida of insisting on distinctions being rigorous if they are to function *as* distinctions (Searle thinks this is an overly demanding requirement), Derrida is utterly incredulous that any *philosopher* would think that this constitutes an unjustifiable demand. How should distinctions function for a philosopher if not rigorously?

Among all the accusations that shocked me coming from [Searle's] pen . . . why is it that this one ["unless a distinction can be made rigorous and precise, it isn't really a distinction at all"] is without doubt the most stupefying, the most unbelievable? And, I must confess, also the most incomprehensible to me? . . . What philosopher ever since there were philosophers, what logician ever since there were logicians, what theoretician ever renounced this axiom: in the order of concepts (for we are speaking of concepts and not of the color of clouds or the taste of certain chewing gums), when a distinction cannot be rigorous or precise, it is not a distinction at all.[52]

Now, it would seem that the entire weight of Derrida's writings on the question of the animal lies on the side of demonstrating, as rigorously as possible, that the human-animal distinction—as it has been drawn by philosophers and the dominant institutions and discourses that employ this traditional distinction—does not hold rigorously at either an ontological or ethical level. If this is the case, then it follows that what is required is the development of alternative ontological and ethical concepts[53] that open up new possibilities for thought and practice. And, true to this line of reasoning, Derrida offers just such a concept at the end of "The Animal That Therefore I Am." In a play on Nietzsche's autobiographical text, *Ecce Homo,* Derrida speaks in his essay (presented at a conference entitled "The Autobiographical Animal") of the "*animot.*" Rather than beholding "the man," Derrida encourages us to behold the *animot, ecce animot.* Why this particular neologism, "*animot*"? First, *animot* sounds like *animaux,* animals in the plural. Derrida wants us to hear in the term *animot* animals in their plural singularity rather than their generality (i.e., The Animal). To behold, and even be struck and wonder about, this plurality of forms, modes, and relations of animal life is one of the events that the philosophical tradition has worked consistently and persistently to block. The neologism *animot* also contains within itself the word for word, "*mot*"—and it is this word for "word," the word as such, which is to say language and access to the being of beings, that has traditionally been denied to animals. Derrida has no interest in trying to persuade his readers that animals do, in fact, have human language (whether certain animal species are capable of human language is an empirical question that Derrida does not take up at any significant length). But he *is* interested in arguing that the "lack" of human language among animals is not in fact a "lack" or privation. To think difference privatively, which is the dominant way of thinking found in Heidegger's and Levinas's discourse on animals, is the dogmatic and anthropocentric prejudice that Derrida's work on the question of the animal is aimed at overcoming.

And yet, despite the destabilization of the human-animal distinction on the proto-ethical level; the contestation of this distinction on the ontological level; and the development of an alternative concept and thought of "animality" as "*animot*"—despite all of this, Derrida resolutely refuses to abandon the human-animal distinction. Now, the reasons for this refusal are rather complicated, and I will attend to them in due course. But I want to note up front that I take Derrida's insistence on maintaining the human-animal distinction to be one of the most dogmatic and puzzling moments in all of his writings. And I am measuring my words carefully here, for Derrida's writings (despite whatever shortcomings they might have) are rarely dogmatic. But I believe that on this particular issue, the criticism is apt. Before examining the reasons behind Derrida's refusal, allow me to cite three representative passages from his work on the issue of the human-animal distinction. The first is from the "second hypothesis" presented in "The Animal That Therefore I Am":

> I won't take it upon myself for a single moment to contest that thesis [i.e., the thesis of "philosophical or common sense" that there is a limit between human beings and animals], nor the rupture or abyss between those who say "we men," I, a man, and what this man among men who say "we," what he *calls* the animal or animals. I won't take it upon myself for a single moment to contest that thesis, nor the rupture or abyss between this "I-we" and what we *call* animals. To suppose that I, or anyone else for that matter, could ignore that rupture, indeed that abyss, would mean first of all blinding oneself to so much contrary evidence; and, as far as my own modest case is concerned, it would mean forgetting all the signs that I have sought to give, tirelessly, of my attention to difference, to differences, to heterogeneities and abyssal ruptures as against the homogeneous and the continuous. I have thus never believed in some homogeneous continuity between what calls *itself* man and what *he* calls the animal. (*AIA*, 398)

The second passage is drawn from Derrida's conversation with Elisabeth Roudinesco. With regard to the division or distinction drawn between human and animal (a division to which Roudinesco says she is "attached," in the sense of believing that it exists and defending the right to insist on this division against animal rights thinkers who destabilize or efface it), Derrida notes that he speaks

> not only of *one* division [between human and animal], but of several divisions in the major modes defining animal cultures. Far from erasing limits, I recalled them and insisted on differences and heterogeneities. . . . Like you [i.e., Roudinesco], I believe that there is a radical discontinuity between what one calls animals . . . and man.
>
> (VA, 72–73)

Elsewhere in the same interview, Derrida adds the following remarks that further develop these points:

> If I am unsatisfied with the notion of a border between two homogeneous species, man on one side and the animal on the other, it is not in order to claim, stupidly, that there is no limit between "animals" and "man"; it is because I maintain that there is more than one limit, that there are many limits. . . . The gap between the "higher primates" and man is in any case abyssal, but this is also true for the gap between the "higher primates" and other animals.　　　　　(VA, 66)

As these passages make abundantly clear, Derrida believes that there is a definitive division, or rather a series of divisions, between human beings and animals. And not only are there divisions here, but *insuperable* divisions, with Derrida going so far as to say that there is a "rupture," an "abyss," and a "radical discontinuity" separating human from animal. Readers familiar with Derrida's "*Geschlecht*" essays, and in particular with the essay "*Geschlecht* II: Heidegger's Hand," will find themselves scratching their heads while reading these claims. In that essay, Derrida took Heidegger to task for insisting on an abyssal rupture between human and animal and for failing to provide any kind of serious scientific and empirical discussion to support the claims of an abyssal rupture.

Is Derrida not doing precisely the same thing here? What evidence is given in support of the claim that there is a rupture or abyss between human and animal? To be sure, "so much contrary evidence" is mentioned, but the contrary evidence is never presented systematically in this essay or anywhere else in his writings. And why not? What would happen if this evidence were presented systematically and opened up to critical analysis? Could it not, then, be critically interrogated, as I have done throughout this book (and using many of Derrida's own arguments!), to the point where the distinction and distinctions drawn between human and animal were seen as (at best) clumsy at an empirical, ethical, and ontological level and dangerous and pernicious at the political level? Might it be that this contrary evidence, if subjected to rigorous analysis across several registers might render it impossible to make a *rigorous* human-animal distinction impossible?

So where, precisely, are these divisions supposed to lie? Derrida has himself cast doubt on the idea that any of the traditional "propers" of the human can be said rigorously to belong to the human alone, but he does *not* conclude from this demonstration that "we must renounce identifying a 'proper of man'" (*VA*, 66). But if none of the traditional "propers" of man (language, consciousness, society, tool use, etc.) hold rigorously, what can be offered in their place? Does Derrida have another way of drawing the human-animal division that is more compelling?

In the texts that are presently available, no such redrawing is to be found. Consequently, it is impossible to know precisely how Derrida's thought would have proceeded along these lines. My guess is that had he sought to carry through on the task of specifying a more elaborate, differential, and refined thought of the human-animal distinction, he would have focused primarily on the manner in which human beings assume (whether negatively or affirmatively) their radical finitude. In other words, the differences between human beings and animals would likely have been sought in the specific modes of responsivity and responsibility (in other words, in the experience of the affirmation or negation of exposure) that Derrida seems to believe are characteristic of and specific to human beings.

But the issue of whether Derrida's reliance on the rhetoric of abysses and ruptures between human beings and animals could be given further justification is ultimately beside the point. The more interesting question is why he would use this language of ruptures and abysses when the largest bodies of empirical knowledge we have concerning human beings and animals strongly contest such language. Heidegger's discourse on abysses and ruptures between human Dasein and animal is, as I showed in the first chapter, openly aimed at contesting Darwinism and the evolutionary theory of his day. Is the same true of Derrida? Is Derrida suggesting that biological continuism is fundamentally mistaken? He is critical (and rightly so, in my estimation) of the sort of biolog*istic* continuism that reduces all discourse on human beings and animals to a biological perspective. But how far does this criticism of biologism extend? Does it entail abandoning a naturalistic framework for explaining the relations and differences between human beings and animals? And if it does not (and, to be clear, I do not think Derrida is antinaturalist in the way that, say, Heidegger or Levinas are), how are we to understand the rhetoric in his texts of abysses and ruptures between human beings and animals and among animals themselves? What function is this language supposed to have?

If Derrida's discussions are aimed at a "productive logic" of the sort that Heidegger pursues, then the contestation of continuism would make a certain amount of sense. Perhaps Derrida's arguments are ultimately aimed at reorienting the sciences in the direction of a more subtle and refined ethical and ontological perspective. However, once again, Derrida's texts on the question of the animal are extremely vague in terms of their ultimate stakes in relation to the sciences, so it is impossible to know for certain what his aims are here. Regardless of his intentions, I think Derrida's insistence on maintaining and reworking the human-animal distinction is profoundly mistaken.

Contemporary thought on this issue must, it seems to me, resolutely refuse the comfort and familiarity of the human-animal distinction and begin instead from the perspective that Donna Haraway gives voice to in her essay "A Cyborg Manifesto":

> By the late twentieth century . . . the boundary between human and animal is thoroughly breached. The last beachheads of uniqueness have been polluted if not turned into amusement parks—language, tool use, social behavior, mental events, nothing really convincingly settles the separation of human and animal. And many people no longer feel the need for such a separation.[54]

I will return to this last sentence. For the moment, I should say that I do not think there is any need to worry, as Derrida seems to, that the kind of position outlined here by Haraway (a position that is informed by developments in both the humanities and empirical sciences and that proceeds from a commitment to both naturalism and ethical and political progressivism) leads necessarily to a simplistic, biologistic continuism that completely homogenizes animals and human beings. Viewed in this light, Derrida's thought on animals appears to proceed as a solution to a false dilemma. We are presented with only two options: either we think of human beings and animals as separated by a single indivisible line (classical philosophical discourse) or we efface the distinction between human and animal altogether and risk lapsing into a kind of reductive homogeneity (biologistic continuism). His solution to this false dilemma is to maintain human-animal differences by refining, complicating, and reworking the human-animal distinction. But there is another option available beyond philosophical dualism, biologistic continuism, and Derrida's deconstructive approach. This other direction is hinted at by Haraway in the last sentence of the above citation: "many people no longer feel the need for such a separation." In brief, *we could simply let the human-animal distinction go* or, at the very least, not insist on maintaining it. Even if one agrees with Derrida that the task for thought is to attend to differences that have been overlooked and hidden by philosophical discourse, this does not mean that *every* difference and distinction that guides common sense and philosophy should be maintained and refined. Might not the challenge for philosophical thought today be to proceed altogether without the guardrails of the human-animal distinction and to invent new concepts and new practices along different paths?

NOTES

INTRODUCTION: THE QUESTION OF THE ANIMAL

1. A helpful discussion concerning the difficulties associated with classical taxonomies and recent alternative work in cladism can be found in Marc Ereshefsky, *The Poverty of the Linnaean Hierarchy: A Philosophical Study of Biological Taxonomy* (Cambridge: Cambridge University Press, 2001). For a general overview of recent debates concerning species essentialism from an interdisciplinary perspective, see Robert A. Wilson, ed., *Species: New Interdisciplinary Essays* (Cambridge, Mass..: MIT Press, 1999).

2. Alain Badiou, *Polemics,* trans. Steve Corcoran (London: Verso, 2006), 106.

3. Although I do not touch on their work here, I should note that the thoroughgoing critique of anthropocentrism in the writings of Graham Harman and Ray Brassier accomplishes at an ontological level what I am trying to effect at the ethical and political levels. I hope to engage with their work more carefully elsewhere. See especially Graham Harman, *Guerilla Metaphysics: Phenomenology and the Carpentry of Things* (Chicago: Open Court, 2005), and Ray Brassier, *Nihil Unbound: Enlightenment and Extinction* (Palgrave MacMillan, forthcoming).

1. METAPHYSICAL ANTHROPOCENTRISM: HEIDEGGER

1. Martin Heidegger, *Being and Time,* trans. John Macquarrie and Edward Robinson (New York: Harper and Row, 1962).

2. Heidegger, *Being and Time,* 100.

3. Heidegger, *Being and Time.*

4. Heidegger, *Being and Time,* §§46–53.

5. Jacques Derrida, *Aporias: Dying—Awaiting (One Another at) the Limits of Truth,* trans. Thomas Dutoit (Stanford, Calif.: Stanford University Press, 1993). Cf. also Gilles Deleuze's remark, "it is the animal who knows how to die, who has a sense or premonition of death" ("Literature and Life," trans. Daniel W. Smith and Michael A. Greco, *Critical Inquiry* 23 [Winter 1997]: 226. For a strong critique of the anthropocentric prejudice concerning the supposedly unique human relation to death, see Allan Kellehear, *A Social History of Dying* (Cambridge: Cambridge University Press, 2007), 11–15.

6. Heidegger, *Being and Time,* 30.

7. Martin Heidegger, *The Fundamental Concepts of Metaphysics: World, Finitude, Solitude,* trans. William McNeill and Nicholas Walker (Bloomington: Indiana University Press, 1995); cited henceforth in the text as *FCM.*

8. Various elements of such a reading, a reading that is more charitable than the one I offer here, can be found in William McNeill's scholarly and remarkably insightful essay "Life Beyond the Organism: Animal Being in Heidegger's Freiburg Lectures, 1929–30," in *Animal Others: On Ethics, Ontology, and Animal Life,* ed. H. Peter Steeves (Albany: SUNY Press, 1999), 197–248. See also Frank Schalow, "Who Speaks for the Animals? Heidegger and the Question of Animal Welfare," *Environmental Ethics* 22 (2000): 259–71, and Stuart Elden, "Heidegger's Animals," *Continental Philosophy Review* 39 (2006): 273–91.

9. The literature on this topic is enormous, but I would recommend in particular Iain Thomson's fine article "Heidegger and the Politics of the University," *Journal of the History of Philosophy* 41 (2003): 515–42.

10. I will not take up the question here of whether Heidegger offers a plausible reading of Nietzsche's will to power, but I will say, without having the space to offer any sustained argument in support of my position, that I think Heidegger's reading of Nietzsche on this issue is dripping with bad faith. It is only through considerable contortion and deliberate misreading of Nietzsche's texts that one can turn his concept of will to power and his concomitant criticism of the hyperbolic naïveté of human chauvinism into subjectivism and neohumanism.

11. Martin Heidegger, *Nietzsche,* vol. 4, *Nihilism,* ed. David Farrell Krell (New York: Harper and Row, 1982), 147.

12. Martin Heidegger, *Parmenides,* trans. André Schuwer and Richard Rojcewicz (Bloomington: Indiana University Press, 1992); cited henceforth in the text as *P.*

13. Friedrich Nietzsche, "On Truth and Lie in an Extra-Moral Sense," in *The Portable Nietzsche,* ed. Walter Kaufmann (New York: Viking Press, 1968), 42; emphasis added.

14. Friedrich Nietzsche, *The Gay Science,* trans. Walter Kaufmann (New York: Vintage, 1974), §374.

15. Nietzsche, *The Gay Science,* §374.

16. Friedrich Nietzsche, *The Will to Power,* trans. Walter Kaufmann and R. J. Hollingdale (New York: Vintage, 1967), 12–14.

17. See Gilles Deleuze and Félix Guattari, *A Thousand Plateaus: Capitalism and Schizophrenia,* trans. Brian Massumi (Minneapolis: University of Minnesota Press, 1987), 240–41.

18. On Kafka and becoming-animal, see Gilles Deleuze and Félix Guattari, *Kafka: Toward a Minor Literature,* trans. Dana Polan (Minneapolis: University of Minnesota Press, 1986).

19. Martin Heidegger, "Plato's Doctrine of Truth," trans. Thomas Sheehan, in *Pathmarks,* ed. William McNeill (Cambridge: Cambridge University Press, 1998), 181.

20. Heidegger, "Plato's Doctrine of Truth," 181.

21. Heidegger, "Plato's Doctrine of Truth," 181.

22. Martin Heidegger, "Letter on 'Humanism,'" trans. Frank A. Capuzzi, in *Pathmarks,* ed. William McNeill (Cambridge: Cambridge University Press, 1998), 245; henceforth cited in the text as *LH.*

23. Jacques Derrida, "The Ends of Man," in *Margins of Philosophy,* trans. Alan Bass (Chicago: University of Chicago Press, 1982), 128.

24. See, among several other places, *FCM,* 264.

25. Derrida, "The Ends of Man," 128.

26. And we should bear in mind that this conception of responsibility can be read in terms of a responsibility to beings beyond man, for example, to animals and other so-called nonhuman entities, to all Others. Indeed, there is a sense in which Heideggerian responsibility might be understood as infinite in a manner that supplements and goes well beyond Levinas's conception of infinite responsibility that I shall examine in the next chapter. For Levinas, responsibility is infinite insofar as it can never be fully assumed or accomplished—something that would render good conscience

impossible. Yet responsibility remains finite within Levinas's work insofar as it is limited to the human alone. Heidegger's conception of responsibility could conceivably be brought to bear on this limitation in Levinas's work. For more on such a project see John Llewelyn, *The Middle Voice of Ecological Conscience: A Chiasmic Reading of Responsibility in the Neighbourhood of Levinas, Heidegger, and Others* (London: Macmillan, 1991).

2. FACING THE OTHER ANIMAL: LEVINAS

1. Emmanuel Levinas, *Of God Who Comes to Mind,* trans. Bettina Bergo (Stanford, Calif.: Stanford University Press, 1998), 177.

2. Emmanuel Levinas, *Difficult Freedom: Essays on Judaism,* trans. Seán Hand (Baltimore, Md.: Johns Hopkins University Press, 1990), 152–53; cited henceforth in the text as *DF.*

3. Emmanuel Levinas, "The Paradox of Morality," portions reprinted in *Animal Philosophy: Essential Readings in Continental Thought,* ed. Matthew Calarco and Peter Atterton (New York: Continuum, 2004), 50.

4. For an extended discussion of Darwin and animal ethics, see James Rachels, *Created from Animals: The Moral Implications of Darwinism* (Oxford: Oxford University Press, 1990).

5. Richard Dawkins, *The Selfish Gene* (Oxford: Oxford University Press, 1976), 2.

6. Dawkins's discussion of "memes" and culture, which are sometimes thought to mark a break from nature, should not be read as a form of human exceptionalism in his work. Dawkins's position on conscious foresight would be a better place in which to mark a rupture between human and animal in his writings, but even that distinction is not at all straightforward.

7. "I am not concerned here with the psychology of motives" (Dawkins, *The Selfish Gene,* 4).

8. Frans de Waal, *Good Natured: The Origins of Right and Wrong in Humans and Other Animals* (Cambrdige, Mass.: Harvard University Press, 1996). Notice, however, that de Waal will not go so far as to endorse animal rights, despite the underlying logic of his position on biological continuism. See the "Conclusion" of *Good Natured.*

9. Emmanuel Levinas, *Totality and Infinity: An Essay on Exteriority,* trans. Alphonso Lingis (Pittsburgh, Penn.: Duquesne University Press, 1969), 64–70, cited henceforth in the text as *TI.*

10. And the nonethicality of things has been questioned, effectively and forcefully, in Silvia Benso, *The Face of Things: A Different Side of Ethics* (Albany: State University of New York Press, 2000).

11. Emmanuel Levinas, "Is Ontology Fundamental?" trans. Peter Atterton, in *Basic Philosophical Writings,* ed. Adrian Peperzak, Simon Critchley, and Robert Bernasconi (Bloomington: Indiana University Press, 1996), 10.

12. In sharp contrast to his later writings, in an early essay Levinas entertains the notion that existence as such can strike one as a miracle. See his "The Meaning of Religious Practice," trans. Peter Atterton, Matthew Calarco, and Joelle Hansel, *Modern Judaism* 25 (2005): 285–89.

13. Levinas, "The Paradox of Morality," 49.

14. Levinas, "The Paradox of Morality," 49.

15. Levinas, "The Paradox of Morality," 50.

16. See Charles S. Brown and Ted Toadvine, eds., *Eco-phenomenology: Back to the Earth Itself* (Albany: State University of New York Press, 2003).

17. Kenneth E. Goodpaster, "On Being Morally Considerable," *Journal of Philosophy* 75 (1978): 308–25.

18. See Mary Anne Warren, *Moral Status: Obligations to Persons and Other Living Things* (Oxford: Oxford University Press, 1997).

19. Thomas Birch, "Moral Considerability and Universal Consideration," *Environmental Ethics* 15 (1993): 313–32, cited henceforth in the text as MC. A significant secondary debate has grown up around this essay. In this regard, see especially Anthony Weston, "Universal Consideration as an Originary Practice," *Environmental Ethics* 20 (1998): 279–89; Jim Cheney, "Universal Consideration: An Epistemological Map of the Terrain," *Environmental Ethics* 20 (1998): 265–77; and Tim Hayward, "Universal Consideration as a Deontological Principle: A Critique of Birch," *Environmental Ethics* 18 (1996): 55–64.

3. JAMMING THE ANTHROPOLOGICAL MACHINE: AGAMBEN

1. Giorgio Agamben, *Language and Death: The Place of Negativity,* trans. Karen E. Pinkus with Michael Hardt (Minneapolis: University of Minnesota Press, 1991), 53.

2. Aristotle, *The Politics,* ed. Stephen Everson (Cambridge: Cambridge University Press, 1996), 1253a 8–18.

3. Gorgio Agamben, *Infancy and History: Essays on the Destruction of Experience,* trans. Liz Heron (London: Verso, 1993).

4. Émile Benveniste, *Problems in General Linguistics,* trans. Mary Elizabeth Meek (Coral Gables, Fla.: University of Miami Press, 1971).

5. Georges Bataille, *Theory of Religion,* trans. Robert Hurley (New York: Zone Books, 1989), 19.

6. Agamben, *Infancy and History,* 51–52.

7. The scientific literature on this topic is enormous. One helpful entry point into the literature is Frans B. M. de Waal and Peter L. Tyack, eds., *Animal Social Complexity: Intelligence, Culture, and Individualized Societies* (Cambridge, Mass.: Harvard University Press, 2003).

8. See Giorgio Agamben, *The Coming Community,* trans. Michael Hardt (Minneapolis: University of Minnesota Press, 1993).

9. Giorgio Agamben, *Means Without End: Notes on Politics* (Minneapolis: University of Minnesota Press, 2000), 92. See also Agamben, *The Coming Community,* 92, for a similar argument about human exceptionalism in politics couched in the terms of the notion of the irreparable.

10. A number of animal species do have an interest in mirrors, and many have even passed the so-called mirror test developed by Gordon G. Gallup Jr. See Clive D. L. Wynne, *Animal Cognition: The Mental Lives of Animals* (New York: Palgrave, 2001).

11. Giorgio Agamben, *Homo Sacer: Sovereign Power and Bare Life,* trans. Daniel Heller-Roazen (Stanford, Calif.: Stanford University Press, 1998), 104–11.

12. Giorgio Agamben, *Remnants of Auschwitz: The Witness and the Archive,* trans. Daniel Heller-Roazen (New York : Zone Books, 1999).

13. Giorgio Agamben, *The Open: Man and Animal,* trans. Kevin Attell (Stanford, Calif.: Stanford University Press, 2004), cited henceforth in the text as O.

14. Agamben, *Homo Sacer,* 11.

15. Agamben, *Homo Sacer,* 10.

16. This question is a variation on a point made by Slavoj Žižek in his dialogue with Judith Butler and Ernesto Laclau. See Judith Butler, Ernesto Laclau, and Slavoj Žižek, *Contingency, Hegemony, Universality: Contemporary Dialogues on the Left* (London: Verso, 2000), 326.

17. Jacques Derrida and Elisabeth Roudinesco, *For What Tomorrow . . .: A Dialogue,* trans. Jeff Fort (Stanford, Calif.: Stanford University Press, 2004), 65.

18. Friedrich Nietzsche, *Will to Power,* trans. Walter Kaufmann (New York: Viking, 1968), §12B.

4. The Passion of the Animal: Derrida

1. Jacques Derrida, "The Animal That Therefore I Am (More to Follow)," trans. David Wills, *Critical Inquiry* 28 (Winter 2002): 369–418; quotation at 402; cited henceforth in the text as *AIA*.

2. Jacques Derrida, *Of Grammatology,* trans. Gayatri C. Spivak (Baltimore, Md.: Johns Hopkins University Press), 244–45.

3. Jacques Derrida, *Glas,* trans. John P. Leavey Jr. and Richard Rand (Lincoln: University of Nebraska Press, 1986), 26.

4. See Derrida's discussion of Benjamin in *AIA,* 388 ff. Beatrice Hanssen, *Walter Benjamin's Other History: Of Stones, Animals, Human Beings, and Angels* (Berkeley: University of California Press, 1998), provides a fuller discussion of the place of animals and nature in Benjamin's work.

5. Jacques Derrida, "Violence and Metaphysics: An Essay on the Thought of Emmanuel Levinas," in *Writing and Difference,* trans. Alan Bass (Chicago: University of Chicago Press, 1978), 142–43.

6. Jacques Derrida, "*Geschlecht* II: Heidegger's Hand," trans. John P. Leavey Jr., in *Deconstruction and Philosophy,* ed. John Sallis (Chicago: University of Chicago Press, 1987), 161–96.

7. Jacques Derrida, *Of Spirit: Heidegger and the Question,* trans. G. Bennington and R. Bowlby (Chicago: Chicago University Press, 1989), chapter 6.

8. See *AIA.*

9. Jacques Derrida, *Aporias: Dying—Awaiting (One Another at) the Limits of Truth,* trans. Thomas Dutoit (Stanford, Calif.: Stanford University Press, 1993).

10. For one example among many, see Jacques Derrida, "'Eating Well,' Or the Calculation of the Subject," in *Who Comes After the Subject?* ed. Eduardo Cadava, Peter Conor, and Jean-Luc Nancy (New York: Routledge, 1991), 116.

11. See, for example, Jacques Derrida, "Force of Law: The 'Mystical Foundation of Authority,'" *Cardozo Law Review* 11 nos. 5–6 (1990): 952–53, and "Violence Against Animals," in Jacques Derrida and Elisabeth Roudinesco, *For What Tomorrow?* trans. Jeff Fort (Stanford, Calif.: Stanford University Press, 2004). 62–76.

12. Jacques Derrida, *The Gift of Death*, trans. David Wills (Chicago: University of Chicago Press, 1995), 69; see also Derrida's discussion of Baudelaire's "Les bons chiens" in *Given Time: I. Counterfeit Money* (Chicago: University of Chicago Press, 1992), 143–44.

13. One final point worth mentioning along these lines is the importance Derrida accords the question of the animal in developing future work in the humanities. On this point, see "The Future of the Profession, or the University Without Condition," in *Jacques Derrida and the Humanities: A Critical Reader*, ed. Tom Cohen (Cambridge: Cambridge University Press, 2001), 50–51.

14. Heidegger, of course, mentions these matters in the context of a contentious comparison between the mechanized food industry and concentration camps—a comparison that, as we shall see, Derrida also makes—but he does not follow it up with the kind of careful historical and ethicopolitical analysis that Derrida provides.

15. Philippe Lacoue-Labarthe, *Heidegger, Art, and Politics*, trans. Chris Turner (Oxford: Blackwell, 1990), 34.

16. For an extended discussion of Isaac Singer, see Charles Patterson, *Eternal Treblinka: Our Treatment of Animals and the Holocaust* (New York: Lantern, 2003).

17. Boria Sax surveys the merits and demerits of various positions on this issue in *Animals in the Third Reich: Pets, Scapegoats, and the Holocaust* (New York: Continuum, 2000).

18. Derrida, "Violence Against Animals"; cited henceforth in the text as *VA*.

19. Gary Francione's most detailed discussion of his incremental abolitionist position can be found in *Rain Without Thunder: The Ideology of the Animal Rights Movement* (Philadelphia: Temple University Press, 1996).

20. Bentham's thinking on animals was considerably more complicated than his more famous textual pronouncements would lead readers to believe. For a fuller discussion, see Gary Francione, *Introduction to Animal Rights: Your Child or the Dog?* (Philadelphia: Temple University Press, 2000), chapter 6.

21. Jeremy Bentham, *An Introduction to the Principles of Morals and Legislation*, ed. J. H. Burns and H. L. A. Hart (Oxford: Oxford University Press), 283 n. 6.

22. See Peter Carruthers, *The Animals Issue: Moral Theory in Practice* (Cambridge: Cambridge University Press, 1992).

23. These themes are broached in Cora Diamond's remarkable essay "The Difficulty of Reality and the Difficulty of Philosophy," *Partial Answers: Journal of Literature and the History of Ideas*, nos. 1, 2 (June 2003): 1–26.

24. One of Derrida's most fecund analyses of the event, invention, and an entire chain of related *"venir"* words can be found in his "Psyche: Inventions of the Other," trans. Catherine Porter, in *Reading de Man Reading*, ed. Lindsay Waters and Wlad Godzich (Minneapolis: University of Minnesota Press, 1989), 25–65. Concerning the classical concept of invention, Derrida notes in this essay (first delivered in 1984) that it has always excluded the animal: "no one has ever authorized himself to say of the animal that it invents, even if, as it sometimes said, its production and manipulation of instruments resemble human invention" (44). The classical concept of invention, and its reinforcement of the supposedly unique human capacity for *techne*, thus allows us another opportunity to grasp the inner connections between anthropocentrism and metaphysical humanism: "This techno-epistemo-anthropocentric dimension inscribes the value of invention in the set of structures that binds differentially the technical order and metaphysical humanism." Derrida goes on to suggest that if we are going to reinvent invention in terms of the advent of the *tout autre*, "it will have to be done through questions and deconstructive performances bearing upon the traditional and dominant value of invention, upon its very status, and upon the enigmatic history that links, within a system of conventions, a metaphysics to technoscience and to humanism" (44).

25. For Derrida's brief discussion of these cat figures, see *AIA*, 376.

26. The passage I am referring to is §352 in Friedrich Nietzsche, *The Gay Science*, trans. Josefine Nauckhoff (Cambridge: Cambridge University Press, 2001).

27. John Berger's well-known essay "Why Look at Animals?" (in his *About Looking* [New York: Pantheon, 1980)] would have us believe that the possibility of encountering the look of another animal is for us today a near-impossibility. The look that used to occur between the human and the animal, he tells us, "has been extinguished. . . . This historic loss, to which zoos are a monument, is now irredeemable for the culture of capitalism" (27). This might lead us to think that Derrida's encounter with the gaze of a household cat is not a genuine encounter with the *Other* animal, but only with the all-too-familiar animal that has "been co-opted into the *family*" (13). Is Derrida's cat just another example of a family pet, one of Deleuze and Guattari's "Oedipalized animals"? (For their tripartite schema of animal kinds, see Gilles Deleuze and Félix Guattari, *A Thousand Plateaus: Capitalism and Schizophrenia*, trans. Brian Massumi [Minneapolis: University of Minnesota Press, 1987], 240–41, and the discussion offered in chapter 1 of the present

volume.) Perhaps not, for this animal, although seemingly familiar, ultimately shatters any attempt on Derrida's part to conceptualize it. Although such an encounter with a domesticated animal would complicate his thesis about the disappearance of animals, even Berger admits that a domesticated animal can "surprise" the human ("Why Look at Animals?" 3). Deleuze and Guattari make the same admission with respect to so-called domestic animals. In view of their distinction among Oedipal, State, and pack animals, Deleuze and Guattari write: "Cannot any animal be treated in all three ways? There is always the possibility that a given animal, a louse, a cheetah or an elephant, will be treated as a pet, my little beast. And at the other extreme, it is also possible for any animal to be treated in the mode of pack or swarm. . . . Even the cat, even the dog." (*A Thousand Plateaus*, 241).

28. Steve Baker, *The Postmodern Animal* (London: Reaktion, 2000), 185.

29. In the afterword to his *Limited Inc.* (Evanston, Ill.: Northwestern University Press, 1988), Derrida addresses the issue of reference in the following terms: "What I call 'text' implies all the structures called 'real,' 'economic,' 'historical,' socio-institutional, in short: all possible referents. Another way of recalling that 'there is nothing outside the text.' That does not mean that all referents are suspended, denied, or enclosed in a book, as people have claimed, or have been naïve enough to believe and to have accused me of believing. But it does mean that every referent, all reality has the structure of a differential trace, and that one cannot refer to this 'real' except in an interpretive experience" (148).

30. Compare Derrida's early essay on the role of madness, philosophy, and reason in Foucault's *Madness and Civilization*: "Cogito and the History of Madness," in *Writing and Difference*, trans. Alan Bass (Chicago, University of Chicago Press, 1978).

31. Tom Regan, "The Case for Animal Rights," in *Animal Rights and Human Obligations*, ed. Tom Regan and Peter Singer (Englewood Cliffs, N. J.: Prentice Hall, 1989). For the full defense of Regan's position, see his *The Case for Animal Rights* (Berkeley: University of California Press, 1983).

32. Regan, *The Case for Animal Rights*, 78.

33. Recall Derrida's remark: "I do not believe in the miracle of legislation" (*VA*, 65).

34. Derrida, "Force of Law," 951.

35. See especially Carol Adams, *The Sexual Politics of Meat: A Feminist-Vegetarian Critical Theory* (New York: Continuum, 1990), and *Neither Man Nor Beast: Feminism and the Defense of Animals* (New York: Continuum, 1994).

36. David Nibert, *Animal Rights/Human Rights: Entanglements of Oppression and Liberation* (Lanham, Md.: Rowman and Littlefield, 2002).

37. Derrida, "Force of Law," 953.

38. Derrida, "'Eating Well,'" 114.

39. Derrida, "'Eating Well,'" 114. There is, of course, the question of Adolf Hitler's purported vegetarianism, which Derrida briefly addresses in a footnote to "'Eating Well'" (119 n. 14). Presently, in the United States, there is at least one exception to this rule: Congressman Dennis Kucinich, who is reported to be a strict vegan and presented himself as a Democratic candidate for the presidency in 2004 and 2008. There is also the example of Dr. Janez Drnovsek, president of Slovenia, who has spoken openly and at length about his vegetarianism.

40. Derrida, "Force of Law," 953.

41. David Wood, "*Comment ne pas manger*—Deconstruction and Humanism," in *Animal Others: On Ethics, Ontology, and Animal Life,* ed. H. Peter Steeves (Albany: State University of New York Press, 1999), 33.

42. Derrida, "'Eating Well,'" 114–15.

43. Derrida, "'Eating Well,'" 114.

44. I have no desire to attack any particular authors for egregious misreadings, although several examples could be given. Rather I will refer the reader to what I take to be one of the more reliable and interesting readings of Derrida's remarks on animals: Cary Wolfe, *Animal Rites: American Culture, the Discourse of Species, and Posthumanism* (Chicago: University of Chicago Press, 2003).

45. Jacques Derrida, *The Politics of Friendship,* trans. George Collins (London: Verso, 1997), chapters 1 and 8.

46. Derrida gives readings of all of these figures in *L'animal que donc je suis* (Paris: Éitions Galilée 2006). The chapter on Lacan in this book has been translated into English as "And Say the Animal Responded?" trans. David Wills, in *Zoontologies: The Question of the Animal,* ed. Cary Wolfe (Minneapolis: University of Minnesota Press, 2003), 121–46.

47. Martin Heidegger, *What Is Called Thinking?* trans. J. Glenn Gray (New York: Harper, 1976), 16; translation modified.

48. Derrida, "*Geschlecht* II," 173.

49. Jacques Derrida, "On Reading Heidegger: An Outline of Remarks to the Essex Colloquium," *Research in Phenomenology* 17 (1987): 183.

50. Elisabeth de Fontenay, *Le silence des bêtes: La philosophie a l'epreuve de l'animalite* (Paris: Fayard, 1998). A short essay from Fontenay on animals

entitled "Like Potatoes: The Silence of Animals" can be found in Christina Howells, ed., *French Women Philosophers: A Contemporary Reader* (London: Routledge, 2004), 156–68.

51. Georges Bataille, *The Accursed Share,* vol. 3, *Sovereignty,* trans. Robert Hurley (New York: Zone Books, 1991).

52. Derrida, afterword to *Limited Inc.,* 123.

53. I am using "concept" in a Deleuzean sense; I am aware that Derrida has registered his unease with the concept "concept" in numerous places and that he would object to this language.

54. Donna Haraway, "A Cyborg Manifesto: Science, Technology, and Socialist-Feminism in the Late Twentieth Century," in *Simians, Cyborgs, and Women: The Reinvention of Nature* (New York; Routledge, 1991), 151–52.

INDEX

abyss, rhetoric of, 22–23, 30–31, 48, 50, 141, 145–48

Adams, Carol, 132

Agamben, Giorgio, 13, 14, 141; animal language, view of, 84–85; anthropocentrism of, 87, 90, 102, 141; anthropological machine, concept of, 92–102; antihumanism of, 87–89; bare life, concept of, 87, 95; coming community, concept of, 92, 95–97, 101; Dasein, view of, 98–100; exposition, concept of, 86–87; infancy, concept of, 80, 82, 85–86; unsavable life, concept of, 100–101; *Works*: "The Face," 86–87; *Homo Sacer* series, 87–89; *Infancy and History,* 82, 85–86; *Language and Death,* 81; *L'aperto: L'uomo e l'animale (The Open: Man and Animal),* 79, 88–102

alterity: of animals, 36, 70, 75; of Other, 11–12, 125–26, 134–36

altruism: among nonhuman animals, 56–59; biological analysis of, 61–62; selfish-gene theory, 60–62. *See also* animal ethics; ethics

Anglo-American philosophy, 108, 114–16, 119

animal activists, as "domestic terrorists," 96

animal ethics, 55–56; environmental issues and, 75–76; extent of, 68; universal ethical consideration, 55, 69–77. *See also* altruism; ethics

animalitas, 44–52, 88

animality, 2–7; world, relationship to, 20–28, 50

Animal Liberation (Singer), 117

animal protection movement, 113–14

animal rationale, 32–35, 45–53

animal rights philosophy, 5–9

animal rights politics, 7–8, 113–14

animals: alterity of, 36, 70, 75; altruism among, 56–59; Being of, on animal's terms, 20–21; communication as fully linguistic, 84–85; fascination for, 42–43; gaze of, 121–26, 159n. 27; as humanized, 93–94; living conditions of, 76–77; plural singularity of, 145–46; privileging of, 35–36; resistance to subjection, 76–77; singularity of, 58, 75, 112, 124–25, 136, 139, 142–44; subjectivity of, 126–36; "what is" and, 34–35

Fundamental Concepts of Metaphysics,
 The (Heidegger), 18–28, 99, 138;
 communal cooperation, concept of,
 19, 23, 26–27, 39; dogmatism of,
 22–24, 27–28, 39; world, concept
 of, 20–28, 50

gaze, of animal, 121–26, 159n. 27
genes, 60–61, 154n. 5
genocides, animal, 111–12
Guattari, Félix, 41–43, 159–60n. 27

Haraway, Donna, 141, 148
Hebrew Bible, animal illustrations,
 91–92
Heidegger, Martin: Agamben's view
 of, 98–100; *animal rationale,* view
 of, 32–35, 45–53; anthropocentrism, reinforcement of, 29–30,
 52–53; anthropocentrism of, 20,
 27–29, 36–37, 138; anthropological
 machine and, 99–100; commonsense notions, analysis of, 20–22;
 communal cooperation, concept of,
 19, 23, 26–27, 39; death, modes of,
 16–17, 138–39; Derrida's view of,
 4, 137–39, 144–46; dogmatism of,
 14, 17, 22–24, 27–28, 39, 45, 138;
 ek-sistence, concept of, 35, 46–53,
 100, 123; essentialism of, 26–27,
 30, 38–39; human-animal distinction, view of, 15, 16–31; *humanitas*
 and *animalitas,* 44–52; influence on
 Continental philosophy, 15, 29;
 mechanized food industry remark,
 110, 158n. 14; Nietzsche, analysis of,
 31–43; nonanthropocentric analysis
 of animal Being, 20–21, 28–29,
 31, 38; privative interpretation of
 animal life, 17–18; world, concept
 of, 20–28, 50; Works: *An Introduc-*

tion to Metaphysics, 100; "Letters
 on 'Humanism,' " 43–52; Parmenides lectures, 33, 39, 99; "Plato's
 Doctrine of Truth," 43–45. *See also*
 Being and Time; Fundamental Concepts of
 Metaphysics
homo humanus, 44
human-animal distinction, 2; as
 abyssal, 22–23, 30–31, 48, 50, 141,
 145–48; altruism and, 56–59; capacities of human and animals, 22,
 35–36, 39, 51, 82, 105, 117–18, 130,
 159; Heidegger's view, 15, 16–31;
 hierarchical versions of, 22–23,
 110–12, 129–31; historical and
 genealogical analysis of, 140–41;
 human-animal homogeneity, 30;
 impossibility of, 143–47; no longer
 needed, 3–4, 149; philosophy and
 science, relationship between,
 18–20; postmetaphysical and, 79;
 rupture in, 63–64; as simplistic,
 105, 139; strategic disruption of
 metaphysical anthropocentrism,
 74–75
humanism, 6, 41; anthropological
 machine and, 92–102; Being and,
 44–45; complicity with dogmatic
 metaphysics, 52–53; hyperhumanism, 48–49; metaphysical, 12–14.
 See also metaphysical humanism;
 ontotheological humanism
humanitas, 44–52, 88
humans: *animal rationale* concept of,
 45–53; as animals having language,
 45, 50–51; biologistic analysis of,
 19–20; Dasein, 17–20, 22–29,
 38, 98–100, 147; as deprived of
 language, 85; as ethical concept, 64;
 limits of, 6; marginalized, 10, 132
hyperhumanism, 48–49

identity politics, 7–10
incrementalist approach, 97
infancy, concept of, 80, 82, 85
inherent value, 100, 111
interests of animals, 7, 74
interruption, 5, 64–70, 73–74, 90, 106, 117–18, 120; kinds of, 70–71
intersubjectivity, 82–83
Introduction to the Principles of Morals and Legislation (Bentham), 116–20
invention, 159n. 24

justice, deconstruction as, 133–34

Kafka, Franz, 42–43
knowledge, perspectival character of, 40–41
Krell, David, 48

Lacoue-Labarthe, Phillipe, 82, 110
language, 143; animal communication as fully linguistic, 84–85; conceptualization, resistance to, 124; human as animal having, 45, 50–51; humans as deprived of, 85; political and social life and, 80–82; subjectivity constituted by, 82–84; Voice and, 81–82; *zōon logon echon,* 45, 50
left, fragmentation of, 6–8, 10
legal institutions, limits of, 127–29, 131
Levinas, Emmanuel, 5, 12, 14; agnosticism of, 68–71, 74; animals incapable of ethical response, 55–56; anthropocentrism of, 62–64; Darwin, view of, 59–62; Derrida's essay on, 104; dog in concentration camp story, 57–59; face of the Other, 5, 62–63, 67–68, 71, 105, 118–21; politics and ethics in work of, 90–91; universal consideration, concept of, 69–77; Works: "Is

Ontology Fundamental?" 67; "The Paradox of Morality," 67–68; *Totality and Infinity,* 59, 64–67
linguistic idealism, 3
logos, 45

madness, 125
marginalized humans, 10, 132
mechanized food industry, 110, 158n. 14
metaphysical anthropocentrism, 11–13; of Levinas, 62–63; from metaphysical humanism to, 43–53; reversal of, 33–38, 40; strategic disruption of, 74–75
metaphysical humanism, 43–53; *humanitas* and *animalitas,* 44–52, 88
metaphysics of presence, 11–12, 129–31
metaphysics of subjectivity, 11, 129; will to power and, 32–33, 152n. 10. *See also* subjectivity
missing link, 93
modernity, subject of, 12
moral considerability, 70–73
"Moral Considerability and Universal Consideration" (Birch), 72–73
moral philosophy, 8–9
moral standing of animals, 5–6

nakedness, human cognizance of, 111–23
Nancy, Jean-Luc, 82
narcissism, human, 104–5
natural selection, 60–61
Nazis, 31, 87–88; Holocaust, comparison of animal slaughter with, 110–11
neohumanism, 87, 90, 95–97
Nietzsche, Friedrich, 31–43; biological reading of, 31–32; on infinite interpretations, 40–41; reversal of

Nietzsche, Friedrich (*continued*)
human-animal distinction, 32–35,
40; will to power, 32–33, 152n. 10;
Works: The Gay Science, 40–41; "On
Truth and Lies in a Nonmoral
Sense," 39–40
nihilism, 41, 52
nonanthropocentric thought: in Agamben, 90, 141; in Derrida, 10, 13;
in Heidegger, 20–21, 28–29, 31, 38;
in Levinas, 62–64

Oedipal animal, 42, 58, 159–60n. 27
ontotheological humanism, 30;
anthropocentric dimensions of,
104–6, 112, 121, 136
open, the, 33–35
Other: as always human, 55, 64–67;
animal, gaze of, 121–26, 159n. 27;
animal face of, 62–63, 67–68, 105,
118–21; being-for, 56–57, 61, 69;
calls egoism into question, 64–66,
118–19; ethical response to, 55; face
of, 5, 71, 118; impossibility of nonviolent relation to, 135–36; recognition, dialectic of, 125–26; resistance
to, 66–67; Same-Other relation,
64–65, 106; universal consideration
and, 69–77

pack animal, 42, 159–60n. 27
philosophy: of animal rights, 5–9;
faced by animal, 62–63; moral,
8–9; role in animal studies, 4;
science, relationship with, 18–20;
thinking at limits of, 113–14. *See also*
Continental philosophy
Plato, 43–44
political and legal institutions, anthropocentric constraints on, 7–8

politics: of animal rights, 7–8, 113–14;
exposition and, 86–87; identity politics, 7–10; language and, 80–82;
subjectivity and, 82–83
Politics (Aristotle), 80–81
postphenomenological discourse, 12
presence, 67; metaphysics of, 11–12,
129–31; self-presence, 104, 129
presubjective thought, 10, 89–90
privative interpretation of animal life,
17–18, 144–45
pro-animal discourse, reliance on
anthropocentric models, 126–28
propriety, 49, 51, 79, 86

question of the animal, 2, 4–6, 20;
anthropological machine and,
96–97; proto-ethical dimension
of, 17, 58, 108, 116–21, 125–27, 137,
142, 145; as response to interactive
encounter, 117–18

ratio, 45
recognition, dialectic of, 125–26
reference, 160n. 29
Regan, Tom, 8, 114, 130
respect, 108, 114
responsibility, 52, 70, 153–54n. 26
responsivity, 52, 62, 69, 106, 147
rights approach, 108
Rilke, Rainer Maria, 33–43; reversal
of human-animal distinction,
35–36, 40
Roudinesco, Elisabeth, 114, 127,
145–46

Same-Other relation, 64–65, 106
science: accounts of animals, 5–6; biological sciences, 37, 39; philosophy,
relationship with, 18–20